Playing Chase with God

Chris Morgan

Copyright © 2023 by Chris Morgan

All rights reserved.

This book was written by a human, no AI was used.

First Edition 2023

Cover by Alex Watson. You are a legend.

Many thanks for the editing efforts of my friends: Barbara Davidson, Annie Brannon, and Jon Joiner

Jmo: Thank you for all your work on the audiobook. You are one of the most talented people I know. It was a very generous gift of many hours.

Thanks to Nick Kirk for the friendship loan of quality gear for the audio book recording and for the 1,000 music conversations over the years.

Contents

Dedication

Introduction

Section One: Start

1) Show Up
2) Open Up

Section Two: Stay

3) Protect Momentum
4) Start Listening
5) Keep Rhythm

Section Three: See it Through

6) Hike the Distance
7) The Journey of Maturity
8) Everybody

Endnotes

About the Author

Mary Anne

Patient with me through the years as I chase to hear the voice of God. Fellow chaser of the King. My love.

Kmo, Amo, Jmo

I think about you all the time. You are each unique and the treasure of my heart. My daughters and my son. May the rhythms of this book lead you to the face of God.

Mom

You patiently built trust with me through your unfailing love. Therefore, when you talked about prayer, I believed you. When life got difficult, as it always does, I believed that if prayer worked for you then I would try it. God did the rest. Thank you for modeling the Way.

Pastor Kevin Myers

You've said many amazing things over the years, but mostly I learned from watching you chase God. Thank you for a partnership in ministry that has spanned decades. We've seen things together that no one could ever forget. Thank you for inviting me along for the ride.

Introduction

When God is chased, he gets caught.[1]

It's just that simple. Like the whole meaning of life answered in the drama and delight of a children's game. The game? *"Play chase."* When my three children were in those magic ages between three and ten, I would come home from work, and joy would erupt from them like fireworks.

"Daddy!!"

I barely had time to sit down and rest my tired feet. I was the center of their attention and the source of a great celebration. It was the most prized portion of my day. Everyone loved this. Mary Anne loved to have a break, my children loved the fun, and I loved their affection. It didn't take long for them to petition me for games.

Play Chase came in several varieties, you know what I mean — Hide and Seek, Tag, or sometimes just running circles around the couch. But the name says it all: it involved me chasing them or them chasing me. But they were too young to keep up with me. I could easily have hidden beyond their capacity to find me. But I was delighted to let myself be caught by them. Nothing compares with the amusement of a child. Their magical laughter filled the atmosphere. God treats me the same way. When I chase him, he allows himself to get caught.

The chase happens in the unscripted rhythms of the relationship. By this, I mean that while relationships are entirely predictable, they are nevertheless unscripted. They have rhythms and repeated patterns, but there is no outline, no step-by-step recipe for how they work. It's the engagement of the heart one day at a time, lesson upon lesson learned day by day, week to week, until weeks turn into years. The building of a story. A history built on personal interaction and layered discovery.

Prayer is like this.

God designed prayer to be a relational pursuit. However, as strange as it sounds, most of us do not think of prayer as relational. It's often considered a religious duty or moral obligation, something to check off a to-do list rather than something that points me to a personal God.

Yet, prayer persists worldwide. The sharpest of godless philosophies haven't erased the fact that most earth dwellers call out to God at some point. In the northernmost outposts of human existence, you'll find people praying. In every nation, tribe, and tongue, prayer endures. Humanity aims prayers at dark ceilings and hopes to be heard. Sometimes grateful prayers for the miracle of life. Sometimes thankfulness for our colorful existence on earth. At other times, anxiously looking for an explanation from the realm beyond the stars for what we feel. There seems to be a way that life was meant to be, and this is not it. We want somebody to take responsibility and explain what it's all about. Prayers ring out dissatisfied, "Somebody up there, please help us." These prayers flow from different felt needs, but they have one thing in common: they are all distant from God. This is the problem - We are trying to work out our wounds, but in our felt experience of prayer, God seems far away.

Jesus paints a different picture. With him, prayer is personal. God is close, and the experience of prayer is intimate. He calls God "Father." He draws direct lines between his prayers and his actions. He emerges from time spent alone with God able to see what God wanted to do in his immediate surroundings. Then he invites us to do the same.

Jesus did not say, *"Don't try to do what I've been doing; it's way out of your league. Just write down what I've said and done and talk about it for a few thousand years. I'll eventually come back."*

No, instead, he invites me to join him, to do what he did, aim high, pray always, and join heaven's business. Just like on earth, where a thousand strands of shared experience define the strength of a relationship, God invites me to himself. Prayer is the front door to a personal encounter with him, not once or twice, but as the consistent tone and experience of my life. It is a learn-by-doing endeavor. We ask and keep asking. We seek till we wear out a path. We knock, but not politely. We pound on heaven's door with a fist—the fist of prayer. If a fist seems to lack humility, then keep reading.

Who would look at the ocean's surface and think they'd seen all its secrets? Only the one who is not that interested. The one who is content to skim will find the surface of the ocean sufficient to claim familiarity. But in fact, the ocean covers 70% of the planet, and only 5% of it has been explored. The surface is only a minuscule portion of the whole. However, the surface requires the least amount of effort to experience. For many, surface prayers will be enough. For the deeply hungry, more awaits. Only a fraction of the whole has been explored. This book hopes to be your submarine tour guide into prayer exploration that goes deeper into the relational experience than perhaps you've been before.

My father was a high school basketball coach.[2] Over the years of watching his teams, I learned that championship teams are built from the fundamentals. The team that executes in the small details is the most likely to win. Games are indeed won by scoring more points than your opponents, but the wise coach looks at the scoreboard only out of the corner of his eye while keeping a steady gaze on the execution of the building blocks of the game. To win the game, you must outscore the other team, but when you get most of the rebounds and never commit a turnover—the scoring begins to take care of itself. The wins start to build. Prayer is like this also. The fundamentals drive the result.

Unlike basketball, where the fundamentals are about mental and physical excellence, prayer is about relational engagement that is highly intentional and attentive to the details. Like most conversations about fundamentals, they are not complicated. The challenge of doing the fundamentals is not whether you can understand them; it's whether you can sustain them. Do them over and over.

It's not just about **starting**— it's about **staying in** and then **seeing it through**.

This book is not a 'how to' about prayer (though many practical bits of help are included). It is written to shine a light on the essential DNA of prayer. It's about how to see prayer, what makes it work— how to think for yourself and take action. It is not an exhaustive work on prayer any more than a roadmap is designed to tell you all the right places to stop on your trip. It is written to inspire you to engage God personally. To point out the path. The details of your own journey with God are not for me to write; they are yours to live.

When my kids were young and we played chase, they learned how to catch me. They became familiar with my hiding places. I may have been hiding, but I was bursting with the anticipation of being found by them. It was their desire for me and their effort to find me that made it dear. It never got old. Each time was like eternity wrapped inside a moment. So it is with me and God in prayer. When God is chased, he lets himself get caught.

Section One: Start

Every journey has a beginning.

Chapter 1
SHOW UP

Nothing magical can happen until you do

I had 45 minutes before the next meeting on my calendar. I was feeling out of sorts with recent events beyond my control. There were changes raining down upon my life, and I couldn't escape the angst. I couldn't sigh deep enough to dispel the feeling.

I decided to go to an empty part of the church building to be alone with God. I would take the complaint of my soul and push it up against the wall of heaven. I would do the only thing I knew to do when I could do nothing else: pray.

Sometimes the first steps are the hardest ones, but when you are hurting, the prayer door seems wider. The weight upon me was too heavy for me to manage alone. I needed God, so I slipped away unnoticed.

It was a small room. Maybe 30 by 20 on its proudest day. But just big enough for me to walk in circles and not feel silly from my perpetual right-hand turn. It didn't take long to find words. I greeted the Lord out loud and began a combination of admiration and angst. Worship fell from my lips in admiration, but several sentences in I began to tell him how I was really feeling. I walked around the perimeter of the room, each circle opening the layers that I needed to process. I told him that I was impressed and fascinated by him, but I didn't approve of the season I was in. I didn't do too much editing; I just let the honest feelings roll. About 10 minutes went by. What happened next, I cannot explain. I can only try to tell.

As if stepping into a spotlight, I stepped into God's presence. A level of intensity unlike anything I'd ever experienced. As if a cosmic switch had been turned on, I stepped into awe, sensing his holiness and his matchless glory. Like a great startle, my breath was snatched away. My pulse shifted into overdrive. My words lost their ability. I continued to make sentences of prayer, but there were no words big enough to capture the One I was experiencing. A display of power. The tiniest glimpse of his majesty unleashed upon me. I kept trying to form sentences, but every combination of words fell short. Like trying to throw a rock from the valley floor to the top of the mountain, my best efforts fell back to earth, unable to reach the necessary height. Eventually, I settled on repeating the best words my earth-bound soul could muster. I just repeated over and over the words "Holy," "Worthy," and "Hallelujah."

I had been praying about my role as a pastor. For months I'd given myself to praying for a revival-sized move of God's Spirit in the church, in the region, in the nation, and beyond. I'd always been taught that leaders go ahead of the crowd and build bridges, and because I dared to consider myself a spiritual leader, I was praying about building bridges for others to experience God's presence. But His words came to me clear.

"You will not lead anything, but I am coming forth."

Like most people who encounter his voice, I did not hear with my physical ears. But his words were clear, and I had no doubt that it was him. There was no condemnation aimed at me. It was a statement of intent. Clear, powerful, and incredibly humbling.

The bridge I'd been praying about earlier actually appeared into my mind's eye. It was no longer just a metaphor. Now I could see it, in a mental vision. It was a bridge made of wooden boards with a slight semi-circular arc. This was not a bridge I would build; this was a bridge where I'd belong. I wasn't leading anyone across; I was a single plank in its construction. But then I understood that it was a bridge made of prayer, and I was only one of many "boards" laying the floor for the Matchless King to come forth. The leader in me was struck down. In human terms, it seemed like a demotion, but in heaven's economy it was a graduation beyond calculation. Gladly I humble myself to board status if I am one of many who will bear the weight of his presence in the days to come. It is a bridge made of prayer and before we are through, I will ask you to join me.

The whole encounter lasted about twenty-five minutes. It was the most powerful encounter with God I've ever experienced to date. It changed me.

I begin with this story to declare that **we are made for encounters with God**. Moses heard God speak from a burning bush. Noah got instructions for building a giant boat. Enoch walked with God and disappeared from the earth. Paul got knocked to the ground, blinded, and confronted by the voice of Jesus. Isaiah saw God with the train of his robe filling the temple.

Revivalist history tells other stories of encounters not in scripture: John Wesley was "Strangely Warmed" by God's confirming presence at Aldersgate, London 1738. [3] He would go on to play a giant role in the Revival known as the First Great Awakening.

Pastor Charles Finney (1792-1866) wrote in his memoirs:

> "I received a mighty baptism of the Holy Ghost. Without any expectation of it, without ever having the thought in my mind that there was any such thing for me, without any recollection that I had ever heard the thing mentioned by any person in the world, the Holy Spirit descended upon me in a manner that seemed to go through me, body and soul. I could feel the impression, like a wave of electricity, going through and through me. Indeed, it seemed to come in waves and waves of liquid love, for I could not express it in any other way." [4]

From this profound encounter, he rose to become a lightning rod amid the Second Great Awakening Revival.

These are powerful stories. I think we all secretly long for our own burning bush experience. And I believe God intends to grant them. But relationships aren't made of the high points alone. What about the spaces between these highlight moments? The less intense variety of connecting with God? The everyday pursuit? The intentional arrangement of my life (inside and out), so that I can say with an honest and steady gaze— ***"You have my attention."***

It's the forgotten days of devotion that build something relationally priceless. I don't need to chase after radical experiences with God. As I learn to chase God through the long lines of life, radical experiences will inevitably chase me. I can trust that it is God's good nature to lead me toward life-altering encounters. But my efforts are best spent building the habits of intimacy.

All relationships begin in pivotal moments. But the only relationships that thrive are the ones that turn pivotal moments into movements. Romantic sparks turn into a string of dates. Friendship connections turn into friendship activities. In the same way, pivotal moments with God come in all shapes and sizes. Many times, more like a whisper than a shout. Maybe for you, it was a simple nudge in a church service, a moment of conviction at church retreat, or a quiet interaction with the scriptures. God made himself known.

This encounter with God is typically the moment where we make promises to God and ourselves. Our hearts soften, and a lane of open water seems to appear in the spiritual ocean. We decide to follow God more earnestly. It is honest, but it's just a moment. The question is, will that moment turn into an intentional movement in my life? The answer turns out to be the line of demarcation in all important relationships. The relationships that receive intentional investment mature and thrive. The ones who do not fizzle out. This truth stands firm in our desire to chase God: sacred moments must mature into holy movements.

There are many ways to build forward movement with God, but this is a book about prayer. If you've tried to build prayer into your life and lost momentum. If you've never tried and feel too intimidated to start. Maybe you feel like you should start but feel under motivated. Keep reading.

What we all know to be true

Prayer is a relational endeavor. This is good news because there is nothing in your life you've been doing longer than building relationships. All the way back, as you rested in your mother's womb, even then you could likely feel that you were not alone. Somewhere inside the walls of your chest you were already working on the sense of someone else there. It's not surprising that God would take the thing that you've been doing longer than anything else and make it the table of contents for how to pray. Almost everything that prayer requires, you've already been practicing in the normal relational pursuits of your life.

The first clue, then, of prayer is: **Take what you know about building good relationships and apply it to talking to God.**

Am I saying learning to experience God is like dating? Like marriage? Like friendships?

Yes – in a nutshell, I am. Stop reading now if that seems too easy to be true but keep on if you want to demystify prayer.

Now, I'll admit that our relationship with God is unique. For starters, you can't see him, so talking to him is a little weird. But let's be honest, you probably already talk to yourself from time to time. It's no weirder than that. He also knows everything and holds all the authority, so the power dynamic is out of balance. Also, he is holy beyond our ability to express. Matchless in wonder and past finding out. Kind of like talking to the ocean. Nevertheless, the rules of relationship apply. Unlike the ocean, he is personal; he makes himself available to know and be known. That being said, relationships require certain kinds of investment and without those investments, a relationship is impossible. But what kind of investments pay off in prayer? Well . . . the same things that pay off in good relationships.

First, you've got to show up.

I'm not trying to be flippant. I'm not trying to be overly simplistic. It's the kind of simple you can lean on. The kind of simple that's elegant in its power to cut right to the bottom line.

If you want a relationship, you must show up to the relationship.

Like everything else I hope to say in this book, this is not a prayer rule, it's a relationship rule. If you decide to start dating someone, you must set a time and show up. If you start a new job and expect a long and prosperous relationship with the company, you must show up. If you set an appointment with a trainer to get physically fit, you have to show up. Nothing wonderful can happen until you do.

This is so simple that it's easy to take for granted. In fact, when most relationships dry up or run into trouble, it's because somebody stopped showing up. Relationship building in life is hit or miss for us all. Sometimes it works, and we gain a friend. Sometimes we fail, and we lose friends, spouses, family, jobs, or more. We live in an era where we invented a term just to name our lack of ability to show up. It's called ghosting. Don't feel like making plans with your friend? Just don't text back. Don't want a second date? Don't call her. No explanation, no problem. But when the relationship doesn't work, don't act like it's a mystery. It's because relationships take work – they take showing up consistently and often. We feel the consequences of our lack of resolve in loneliness and a trail of broken relationships, but we still struggle to show up.

The same is true for our pursuit of God in prayer. We know the gist of it— talking to God. But we struggle to follow through. We resist the very one we desire to know. We ghost God. Real prayer starts when you show up, and it is sustained by your ability to continue showing up. Obviously, it is way more than just showing up, but you cannot advance to any other base, go any deeper, or travel any further until you are willing to show up. When I say "show up," it can sound trite and casual. Maybe I'll show up, maybe I won't. But that attitude won't get us where we want to go.

Instead of ghosting, the proper posture can be found in Exodus 3. When Moses saw the bush burning, scripture says he "turned aside." He turned from the path normally taken to intentionally go another direction. His decision was not casual but costly and inconvenient. He parked the flock he was watching and walked toward the unknown. Prayer is the same.

Showing up sounds harmless enough, but the truth is, it requires the intentional rerouting of one's life. Be careful of removing the inconvenience of showing up. We live in a world that demands immediate access. *One Minute Prayer Devotionals* lead us toward a mindset of fitting God in. But there is a difference between showing up and fitting in. It is the costly inconvenience that helps us remember we are on holy ground. But when you show up, you are a candidate for something wonderful!

In 1988, Garth Brooks was still undiscovered. Like so many others, he was paying his musical dues, broke and trying to survive. Today he is one of the best-selling music artists of all time. How did he travel from a struggling unknown to a country music hall-of-famer? He showed up.

In April of 1988, Garth Brooks landed an audition with Capitol Records. He played several of his finest songs, but they passed on the young singer-songwriter. In fact, Capital was the seventh record label in a row to turn him down. Just a few weeks later Garth was set to take part in a writer's round at the legendary Bluebird Cafe. He was scheduled to play ninth. Another unsigned artist was booked to play second. The same Capital executives that turned Garth down were there to see the other unsigned artist. The other unsigned artist didn't show up. Garth was asked if he would like to move up into the second slot. He seized the opportunity. He lit up the atmosphere in front of a live crowd. The Capital executives saw something they didn't see before and when the performance was over, they were waiting for him on the side stage. The rest is history.[5]

Garth was on his way to something wonderful, but it started with simply showing up. Relationships begin and are sustained by the power of showing up!

Showing up to what?

"The Kingdom of Heaven at hand" is not just one of Jesus' favorite sayings; it's the true nature of our spiritual opportunity. Prayer is a Jesus-sized door that waves us in. Invited to come and know him. If that sounds predictable in a book about prayer, then slow down for a minute. Don't allow yourself to be so familiar with the language surrounding prayer that you forget to consider its potency. Prayer is the backstage pass to the presence of God. It's personal. God invites us to himself. We have access because of what Jesus has done, but prayer turns that access into experience. Like all our other important relationships— it's not something we do; it's someone we have the privilege to know. There is someone else in the room, and my experience of him is not theoretical hearsay or mere theology; it's actual, like any other fact of my existence.

Because of this, we can leave behind moral obligation and religious duty. Prayer is not required because God demands it. **It's required because it's impossible to know someone personally without talking to them.** To deny prayer its central role in our pursuit of God is like trying to get to the top of the Eiffel tower while ignoring the steps (or elevators). If you wish to experience God – his grace, his mercy, his peace, and all the promises you've heard about – prayer is the front door. We must use it over and over to ascend the heights.

But I'm actually pretty bad at relationships

If you feel inadequate in prayer, then join the club. We all feel that way. When feelings of inadequacy flow from a lack of familiarity (like using unknown technology for the first time or going on a first date), you must press through and remind yourself that it's only a matter of time and these feelings will pass. You confront inadequacy with the certainty that as day adds up upon day you will break through to a different mindset. The way you feel today is valid, but it's not the way you will feel forever. Most relationships begin with a degree of awkward uncertainty. You must continue to show up.

If feelings of humble inadequacy arise from the size of the invitation (an invitation into God's presence), this is a positive indicator that you are clear about the moment to which you are invited. In any version of inadequacy, you can be propelled forward if you choose to see it properly.

We are the club of broken beggars who have been mysteriously esteemed beyond our comprehension and invited to a standing invitation at the King's house. If you don't feel a little overwhelmed at the size of this invitation, then you don't yet realize who you are talking to.

In any case, it's time to stop hiding behind inadequacy and find your voice before the Living God. You are not as lost as you think. You already know more about prayer than you suspect. The path of prayer in front of you is illuminated with shining white stones. These are the relational skills that you've been observing your whole life. But you now must apply them to prayer.If you feel relationally broken (like you are terrible at relationships), don't give up. You are not starting from zero. Slow and steady wins the day.

You may ask, "When you say 'show up', do you mean show up to a devotional place and time for prayer, or are you talking about 'showing up' on the inside where I stay open and communicative with God?" Both, but slow down, we are not there yet. We will talk about both. But just like your earthly relationships, showing up means setting aside specific time but also staying communicative as you go.

Just keep showing up.

Prayer is rich in possibility.

When you are praying, anything is possible. That sounds like the tagline of a show on Christian TV from the 1980s. Very buoyant and a little bit plastic. But if you strip prayer down to its bare bones, the logic of this declaration stands firm. Impossibility is fiction with God. Anything can happen.

"The sun will come out tomorrow; bet your bottom dollar!"[6]

This familiar lyric comes from the Broadway play *Annie*. At first glance, it seems like irrepressible optimism – unreasonable and unrealistic. As the story of Annie plays out, though, it seems more like Annie is aware of a higher story than the rest of us. Like her ear is tuned to a higher conversation than those who are stuck in the "facts" of circumstances. Therefore, we love Annie and the way her story turns out.

Like all great art, the story of Annie is a metaphor for the truest reality.

Annie is an orphan. She treasures pieces of her past (a written note and a locket from her parents). She longs to escape the orphanage, find her parents, and piece her story back together. But she lives under the watchful eye of evil Miss Hannigan.

Just as all seems lost, a woman named Grace appears. She is the assistant to billionaire Oliver Warbucks. Grace invites Annie to his mansion for Christmas. Once in his home, Annie wins his heart. He sees her desire to find her parents and belong. He decides to offer a $50,000 reward to anyone who can prove they are her parents. However, his true heart is to adopt Annie as his own. He begins the legal proceedings privately to make her part of his family.

Meanwhile, the evil Miss Hannigan makes a final effort to ruin Annie's life. Hannigan's unscrupulous brother Rooster and his girlfriend Lily are sent to pose as Annie's real parents. They are armed with the intimate knowledge of the note and the locket as proof that they are her real parents, but the kind Mr. Warbucks does not believe them. At the last moment, there is a surprise visit from the President (FDR: whom she'd met earlier). He has discovered that her true parents died when she was a baby. Rooster and Lily show up and are arrested along with Miss Hannigan for their crimes. Annie is adopted by Daddy Warbucks— the desire of his heart, the desire of hers.

How closely Annie's story resembles our own spiritual story.

Our Heavenly Father's desire is to adopt us, to take us as his own. In accomplishing this, he makes it legal and exposes our enemy. He defeats the one who has pursued us in relentless hatred. His desire all along was to get us into his family. Annie was not operating in blind optimism; she was alive to a higher storyline, a higher conversation. That is what prayer is—a higher conversation. We, who are spiritual orphans, get access to the riches of Heaven through our adoption by the King, our heavenly Father. With him, all things are possible.

Possibility begins with one who will show up.
In 1857 Jeremiah Lanphier, a businessman who lived in New York, gave his life to Christ. Subsequently he was offered a modest position

as a missionary pastor for the Old Dutch North Church at Fulton and Williams streets. Like many other churches who had already thrown in the towel, they were in steep decline. They too considered closing the doors but decided to hire Jeremiah as a last effort. He made very little progress with his door-to-door campaign, until one day, though weary and discouraged, he had a moment of clarity.

An hour for prayer in the middle of the day once a week. Rather than trying to work harder to revitalize the community, he decided to ask God to do the revitalizing work. Take the lunch hour and invite others to show up once a week for prayer. He printed handbills, made personal invitations, and found a room to use. Finally, September 23rd arrived—the noon hour—and nobody showed up.

Undefeated, Jeremiah ascended the steps alone. He prayed by himself for thirty minutes until at 12:30 he heard a single soul climbing the steps. Then another arrived and then another. By the end of the hour there were six who had come to pray. They prayed together briefly, for the hour was almost complete. But they made the key decision to show up again the next week.

When that day arrived, instead of six, twenty showed up. Then the week after instead of twenty there were forty. Jeremiah added bold faith to momentum and decided that they would not only get a bigger room but that they would begin to meet daily. The move was perfectly timed—for what Jeremiah did not know was that a great financial crisis would hit the markets later that same week. The crash closed banks, put men out of work, families went hungry, but the prayer meeting began to explode. Thousands were now attending daily prayer. The newspaper got wind of it and printed a story about the meetings. Within six months, the movement had spread across the city, and 10,000 were gathering daily to ask God to move in their lives. By early 1858 revival power began to spread down south to the Appalachians and into the West until every major town from New York to the Pacific Ocean fell before the movement of God in prayer.

The estimates are that between 300,000 and 1,000,000 people came to faith in Jesus Christ in just a two-year period. Jeremiah Lanphier had hoped to revitalize a community but showed up to pray and saw revival spread to a nation.[7]

Prayer is not powerful when we talk about it, prayer is powerful when we engage God in it. But nothing happens until we show up.

Clearly, when hundreds and thousands of people engage God in prayer, supernatural things begin to happen. But it never begins with the hundreds and the thousands, it begins with the few, or most of the time just the one. This is where we struggle because "the one" means me.

I am the one

I'm the place where prayer breaks down. I am the one whose prayer vocabulary never graduated beyond the children's bedtime status. I am the one who's brilliant at career and hobby but can't muster a portion of my day to pursue knowing God. I am the one who is broken at the core and too proud or too ashamed to admit it. I am the one who needs to root my life in prayer, but the simple truth is, I don't know how. And

I'm too busy to show up so that I can figure it out. To all the "ones" in the world who carry prayer breakdowns, God makes an invitation so simple, a child could understand it.

"Come" (In other words, "Show up.")

> **"Come, all you who are thirsty, come to the waters; and you who have no money, come, buy and eat! Come, buy wine and milk without money and without cost. Why spend money on what is not bread, and your labor on what does not satisfy? Listen, listen to me, and eat what is good, and you will delight in the richest of fare. Give ear and come to me."** (Isaiah 55:1-3, NIV).

Just come.

No covered dish required, no money requested— it's all prepared and paid for, but you must show up. There is no secret handshake— just the humility to come to the table hungry. We get tripped up because we are so aware of what we don't know. We hesitate because we feel incompetent, like someone who's been invited to dinner and though we are hungry, we feel resistant because we don't know the dress code. Hesitance needs to shake hands with humility and embrace the fact that I need the meal more than I need to feel perfectly prepared.

Jesus added:

> "Come to me, all you who are weary and burdened, and I will give you rest. Take my yoke upon you and, learn from me, for I am gentle and humble in heart, and you will find rest for your souls." (Matthew 11: 28-29, NIV).

In the movie "*The Devil Wears Prada,*" Anne Hathaway's character (Andy) is in a crucial conversation with her boyfriend. The tension has been mounting in their relationship, and it has culminated in a moment that will determine their future. Just as the conversation is at its height, Andy's phone rings. It's her boss (played by Meryl Streep). Andy is caught between the desire for her conversation with her boyfriend and the necessity of picking up the call from her boss. Just when she is about to pick up the phone call, her boyfriend delivers the line we need to hear:

"Just so you know, the person whose call you pick up is the one you are in a relationship with."

If I want a relationship with God, then I am going to have to '*pick up his call.*' It's the first rule of a relationship. I have to show up. It's my choice. No proper relationship is ever built on coercion; it's invitation only. Jesus said as much, "Behold, I stand at the door and knock. If anyone hears my voice and opens the door, I will come into him and eat with him and he with me." Revelation 3:20

The day for radical seeking of God is now here and you are more equipped for it than you realize. Start here: show up.

Invocation

It means to invoke something or someone for assistance.

At the end of every chapter an invocation section is offered. This is so we can do more than just talk about prayer. For some this may seem unnecessary, or even trite. Others may be grateful for an additional boost. Take your help as you find it and set your heart to graze wherever you find the greenest pasture.

Next Step:
Set aside time to pray every day and show up.

Scripture:
Come to me, all you who are weary and burdened, and I will give you rest (Matthew 11:28)

Quote:
After decades of night-and-day prayer, I have come to believe that 99 percent of it is just showing up, making the effort to become consciously present to the God who is constantly present to us.

Peter Grieg, founder of a 24/7 prayer movement from "How to Pray (a simple guide for normal people)"

You don't get the awesome reward of walking out of prayer without the challenge of walking in.

Pastor Kevin Myers, 12Stone Founding Pastor

Prayer:
Father,
My life is fast, and many people and things clamor for my attention. Humbly I pause to know you. Quietly I come.

O Jesus, without any answers I draw near. I bring the one thing that you can't find anywhere else— myself.

Open-hearted I come. I know that I need what you give. I also know that it is required of me to show up. Simply to humble myself and acknowledge that I need you. So, just as I am, without excuse, without any other option, I come to you. O Son of God, I come. Not just once do I come to you, but I intend to come over and over until something holy in me is formed. Something dear. Someone dear. I'm seeking your presence and bowing my pride. In the mighty name of Jesus—Amen!

Chapter 2
OPEN UP

Prayer is for closeness with God

When I was a kid, I loved baseball. I remember a scene from a professional baseball game. On this particular day a batter hit a swinging bunt: the accidental maneuver where a batter takes a full swing but catches only a small enough portion of the ball to dribble it into the field of play. Sometimes this turns into an "excuse me" hit. Other times it results in an easy out. On this day the ball rolled politely down the first base line. An easy out.

The first baseman charged the ball and fielded it with ease. The runner ran down the line toward first base. They came face to face on the baseline and both stopped. They apparently knew each other because— without tagging the runner — the first baseman began a conversation. They chatted for a moment standing on the baseline, smiles on their faces, while the rest of the stadium watched. Then the first basemen took the ball he had tucked away in his glove and tossed it to the pitcher. There was an ever so slight but pregnant pause. The runner resumed his run to first base that nobody was covering. The first baseman never tagged him. The runner was safe. The first baseman showed up to field the ball but got distracted and missed the easy out.

Prayer can be like this. We can show up but miss the point. It's possible to show up but never open up to the fellowship of the relationship. It's possible to have the appearance of a relationship without any connection flowing from that relationship. For this reason, we must know the secret of prayer.

The secret to prayer is that prayer is not about prayer. Prayer is about presence.

That means me making a heart connection with God. Not only showing up to speak with God, but my experience of His presence.

Look at it this way.

Prayer is like a ladder. Ladders are generally unimpressive. However, when needed, what else can do what a ladder can? It has no real use except that it assists me in getting to a place that I could otherwise not reach. If you and I were standing in a room full of people and I told you that I had hidden twenty thousand dollars in the ceiling and the first one to find it gets to keep it— at this point a ladder goes from irrelevant to all-important. The ladder under my back porch is a collection place for spiders when it is lying on the ground. But engaged according to its purpose it becomes an indispensable tool. A ladder is fully a means to an end. The clearer I am about this truth concerning prayer, the more appreciative I am of its holy power.

Prayer is the ladder, and the experience of God's presence is the destination. Prayer allows me to plant my ladder right on top of every earthly dilemma and find direction for my soul. The ladder of prayer that is not leaned against the destination of God's presence becomes a discouraging duty and I've entirely missed the point. Prayer must have its outcome understood and achieved or it becomes a tool of the Pharisee; the spiritually busy but completely ineffective.

Prayer is not for religious duty; it is for closeness to God.

But closeness with God is hard to measure. It is intangible. For this reason, it's easy to measure by the clock— as if accumulated time equals intimacy. If I decide that 25 minutes a day is the right amount of time for prayer, but no vital connection is made, then the amount of time doesn't matter, does it? Added up time is the measurement of a religious spirit, but prayer is for relational connection.

So, how do I position my life for the experience of God's presence? For me, it's been a journey, built as I paid attention to what was going on relationally in prayer. Each season has opened up the next layer of understanding. Each insight has expanded my experience of His person. I am a life-long learner, more aware of His acquaintance with every passing year. In a way, every chapter of this book is answering the question, how do I chase the presence of God through prayer? But right here, let me offer a starter kit for opening up my heart to God's presence. This is not an exhaustive list, but they are the pillars that have kept me building a history with God.

Someone there

Loneliness was the first thing that God observed in his creation as "not good" and its eradication is at the very center of the gospel message.

A few years ago, I was staying at a bed and breakfast outside of San Francisco. One evening I fell into a conversation with a stranger who just happened to be a philosophy professor. I don't remember how it happened, but we ended up in a discussion about the existence of God. I was interested in how he addressed the question with his students. He took me through the paces of a couple of arguments they discussed around the *God Question*. I don't remember exactly what I asked next, but I remember his response. He said in a tone that was almost a protest, "That would mean that God is personal." The implausibility of this thought was written all over his face. He isn't alone. Lots of us don't see God as a person. He's more of a postbox to address our prayers to when we need that kind of thing. But if God isn't personal, then prayer is a fool's errand. I know the universe can feel like a lonely and unsympathetic place but the answer to why I pray is simple; I found someone there.

To the one who encounters God, prayer makes sense. I found someone on the other side of the conversation, and prayer was the most direct route to become more acquainted. I've never gotten over the experience of someone there. If God is going to draw near, then I am going to invest to discover him.

Jesus characterizes God as a dwelling God— a Father who has set his sights upon a restored relationship that allows him to make his dwelling with me. The gospel of John 14 is bursting at the seams with this reality. Jesus is preparing to go to the cross and gathers his disciples for their final "locker room speech." And these are the words he chooses:

"Let not your hearts be troubled. Believe in God; believe also in me. In my Father's house there are many rooms... I go and prepare a place for you." (John 14:1 ESV)

We have too often relegated this scripture as speaking of a place to dwell after death. But this falls short of Jesus' invitation. He goes on to prepare his disciples for what was just around the corner: "I will not leave you as orphans; I will come to you." He says further, "the Holy Spirit, whom the Father will send in my name, he will teach you all things and bring to your remembrance all that I have said to you." (John 14:18 and 14:26, ESV)

Jesus is saying that he prepares a place for us in the here and now, and prayer is the door we walk through to get there.

I grew up in a home that believed in prayer, but I never really tried it out for myself until I hit sixteen. That was the year I collided with pain big enough to warrant a prayer test drive. What was the pain? Nothing remarkable. I had fallen in love with a friend of mine and though we were both dedicated to the relationship for the better part of that year, she lost interest. I was young but the pain was real. It was then that I decided I'd try speaking to God on a consistent basis. I noticed the Bible carried some decent-sized promises for the one who would seek God. With my heartbreak in tow, I went to God.

The result was surprisingly quick but not the result I was expecting. I went to God to get the girl, but what I got in return was an awareness of someone else in the conversation. My outward circumstances were not changing, but inwardly I was coming alive to the reality that God was drawing near to me. This changes everything. I prayed because I wanted to escape heartbreak. I have continued to pray because I found God present in the conversation.

AW Tozer speaks of this sense of someone there:

> "The solemn delight that those early disciples knew sprang straight from the conviction that there was One in the midst of them. They knew that the Majesty in the heavens was confronting them on earth: they were in the very Presence of God. And the power of that conviction to arrest attention and hold it for a lifetime, to elevate, to transform, to fill with uncontrollable moral happiness, to send men singing to prison and to death, has been one of the wonders of history and a marvel of the world."[8]

Pray like someone is there: When we do, we pray differently. Employ the rules of real conversation. Imagine if someone were talking to you the way you are praying. Would it make sense? Would it be engaging? Like all relationships, the path of intimate connection in prayer is forged over time and learned through repeated encounters. Also, like all relationships, the degree of felt intensity may wax and wane. Today, more or less than yesterday, but always comforting and self-verifying in the soul. This is the same with all deeper relationships in life. The awareness of closeness goes up and down, but the certainty of the relationship digs deeper with every cycle.

At the center of reaching out for closeness in prayer is your insistence to reject the crushing weight of life by yourself and replace it with the intent to know God by more than hearsay. It requires faith. It requires resolve. It requires undeterred pursuit. But do not think it is all heavy-lifting and spiritual grunt-work. No, the resolved pilgrim steps into prayer but is enriched by communion with God.

"Faith is the road, but communion with Jesus is the well from which the pilgrim drinks." [9]

Tend your flame

God is not withholding his presence from me. In fact, he has made multiple promises to be nearby. But the experience of God's presence doesn't happen to me, it happens through me. In other words, it is reciprocal. If I want his presence, then I must bring mine. If I want his sincerity, then I must bring my authenticity. If I want his heavenly fire, then I must bring my earthly flame. This should not surprise me. All my other important relationships are mutual. Why should mine with God be an exception? It's not. All the relationship rules apply.

My pastor once built a fire on stage. He turned down the lights, stacked up some wood, used a little scout water (lighter fluid), struck a match and the warm glow of a fire set the tone in the room. He gave it 30 seconds to settle into our experience and then he began to teach. He didn't have to say much. Creative metaphors are like that. They did the heavy lifting, he only had to deliver a couple of sentences and we all started absorbing the challenge of the moment.

"Fires deliver lots of energy and heat. But they all burn out if they are left unattended."[10]

In the gospel of the Kingdom, **God lights the fire; we tend the flame.**

In God's ordination of priestly worship in the Jewish Tabernacle there is a responsibility so important that God repeats Himself three times:

The burnt offering is to remain on the altar hearth throughout the night, till morning, and the fire must be kept burning on the altar. (Leviticus 6:9, NIV)

Then again, He says,

The fire on the altar must be kept burning; it must not go out. (Leviticus 6:12, NIV)

Then again, just to be sure,

The fire must be kept burning on the altar continuously; it must not go out. (Leviticus 6:13, NIV)

If I want the experience of God's heart drawing near to mine, then the fire on the altar of my heart must be tended. It must be kept alive. He who is a consuming fire is drawn to my fire. But what does that mean? Fire is a metaphor. What are the actual sources of fuel that need to be watched over in my soul?

◆》・・◆・・《◆

Cultivate Fascination

Fascination with God is the most powerful strategy of the church. Fascination WITH God sparks my fire FOR God, and when I am absent of this intrigue then I am in violation of the code of heaven.

With church gatherings as my filter, I might imagine that God's throne is surrounded by music and sermons. A place where God and those who surround him lightly engage in singing and then sit and evaluate the next communicator, concluding with a golf clap as if someone knocked in a birdie. But compare this to the scriptural scene surrounding God's throne in heaven. Very different. Strange creatures calling out to each other, unwilling to pause.

"Holy, holy, holy is the Lord Almighty; the whole earth is full of his glory." (Isaiah 6:3, NIV)

No golf claps. The doorposts and thresholds shake with the sound of their voices. Spontaneous smoke fills the room, no machines required. Real smoke.

I was in college when I first read *The Lion, the Witch, and the Wardrobe* by C.S. Lewis. Wonder stirred as I read the conversation between the children and the Beavers. Mr. Beaver carried a fascination that was close to the surface. Remember, in this story Aslan is a Lion who is their Creator and soon to be redeemer – clearly a characterization of Jesus Christ.

> "Aslan, a man!" *said Mr. Beaver sternly.* "Certainly not. I tell you he is the King of the wood and the son of the great Emperor-beyond-the-Sea. Don't you know who is the King of Beasts? Aslan is a lion —THE LION, THE GREAT LION." "Ooh!" said Susan, "I'd thought he was a man. Is he — quite safe? I shall feel rather nervous about meeting a lion." "That you will, dearie, and no mistake," said Mrs. Beaver, "if there's anyone who can appear before Aslan without their knees knocking, they're either braver than most or else just silly."

> "Then he isn't safe?" said Lucy. "Safe?" said Mr. Beaver. "Don't you hear what Mrs. Beaver tells you? Who said anything about safe? 'Course he isn't safe. But he's good. He's the King, I tell you." "I'm longing to see him," said

Peter, "even if I do feel frightened when it comes to the point." "That's right, Son of Adam," said Mr. Beaver, bringing his paw down on the table with a crash that made all the cups and saucers rattle. "And so you shall." [11]

Like Peter, my heart quickens with fascination. Like Mr. Beaver, something in me wants to bring my hand down on the table with a crash and say, "I want to meet him!"

When I'm fascinated with him, I'm more ready to meet him.

Reject Passivity

Worship is a verb. It is something I do on purpose. Sometimes my feelings wake up quickly and sometimes not. Either way, I reject a passive stance and put on pursuit. I stretch my outlook heaven high. I pause in wonder and build worship muscle. Honor God for who he is. Remember in gratitude and personal celebration what he has done. This can change the atmosphere all by itself. It slows me down and warms my chilled heart.

Fascination doesn't happen to me; it is cultivated in me. Wake up O Sleeper! Pick up the realities of who God is and stir them into your thoughts, then let words escape from your mouth. Worship words. Fascination doesn't keep company with the casual or religiously bored. To do this successfully, I have to intentionally put off mental drift through stirred wonder.

I pause to ask good questions, muse on delightfully created things, laugh over unsolvable quandaries and mysteries. Be glad to know the One who is high enough to solve all the spinning puzzles. I let my prayers resonate with the proverb writer who says: "There are three things that are too amazing for me, four that I do not understand: the way of an eagle in the sky, the way of a snake on a rock, the way of a ship on the high seas, and the way of a man with a young woman." *(Proverbs 30:18-19, NIV)*

When I look at the world, I am often amazed and wonderfully confused. Prayer is the place to notice and worship the One who sits enthroned above it all. In this lane of prayer, I am both humbled downward and raised up. I loosen my grip on the fixation that I carry about me. I dissolve downward and find my posture as a worshiper. I seek to descend past the cares of my soul and recapture the regal crown of a redeemed and adopted son. I wrap my heart freshly around the reality of my station with God. But make no mistake, worship is work. It happens on purpose.

Those whom I have known over the years who are good at making a worship connection with God are the opposite of passive. They put on worship like a pair of boots for hiking. They refuse to let a detached mindset cause them to miss out. They rarely begin their prayers with their needs, they opt for the lane of prayer that aligns with the praises of heaven. They've learned that this is the kind of prayer that changes the atmosphere of their worries and keeps them hiking further into the experience of God's presence.

Anticipation

All relationships thrive in an atmosphere of eager anticipation. When I expect good things, I approach the conversation differently. I'm upbeat. On the other side of the coin, relationships struggle when interactions become expressionless and dull. Prayer thrives when passion is cultivated. I'm not talking about hype. Hype is counterproductive. Zeal simply means I'm happy to be in this conversation. I'm present and ready to move forward.

I have a friend and mentor, Jack. I've known him for 20 years and he never ceases to be a marvel to me. Jack is a former business owner. He helped run an international company in the tradeshow industry. His stories are a well-spring of wisdom. Over the years I've learned so much from Jack, but the biggest impression he has made upon me is his constant good nature. He is a fountain of belief and encouragement. It never feels contrived. His upbeat approach is not rooted in a super-human personality gift, it is intentional. Deliberate. His encouraging atmosphere draws others toward him. Like a warming fire others gravitate to him to find the warmth of his encouragement.

He once told me that on any random day he would pick three people in his company before he arrived. He would mentally prepare to interact with them and then he would go and initiate a conversation with each one. He would consider their life situations and how he could ask the right questions. He said that he would even practice his smile to make sure that it was authentic. It was at this point that I began to realize that anticipation could be built. It is intentional. I am not a prisoner to my feelings (or lack of them). I can put on an eager expectation like I'm sliding into my favorite coat. The good news is that its habit forming. When you choose this atmosphere, it begins to stick to your personality profile. What I have learned from Jack I apply to prayer. I'm not just showing up to prayer, I'm intentionally reaching out with a chosen demeanor. One that believes. One that invites God to draw near to me.

I'll admit that sometimes the angst of my soul is so keen that I have no choice but to lead out in prayer with a cry for help or even a frustration of disappointment. The Psalms are full of prayers like this. They are a different kind of fire. This is 100% legal and even helpful. Real relationships require honest authenticity.

A uthentic

When Jesus was on earth and he trained his disciples in the way of prayer, he pointed to the religious leaders of his day and said, "You see how those guys pray? Don't do it like that! They pray long memorized prayers. They do it out in the open to be seen by others. Their motives are way off base. They think they are going to be heard because they use so many good sounding words?"[12] Clearly Jesus was not impressed.

Pretense is a relationship killer. Pretense is when I stop saying what I really think and become evasive about how I really feel. I struggle to say what I really want. I start saying what I think God wants to hear instead of just being authentic. If I appear before God without an opinion, then where is the relationship? Why would God invite me to pray except that he wants me – my true thoughts, my honest feelings, my deeply-felt desires? These are the building blocks of real relationships and the true north of effective praying. But it's easy to get caught up listening to the words coming out of my mouth as if valid prayer is supposed to sound a certain way. I shouldn't fret over my sentences; I should let my heart flow. Easy to say, not always easy to do.

There was another day when little children were trying to get to Jesus and the disciples were holding the kids back. "You kids get outta here!" When Jesus noticed what was going on, he said to the disciples, "Don't do that. Let the little children come to me. Don't you realize that the Kingdom of Heaven belongs to such as these? In fact, when you come to God you should come as a little child."[13]

Here's the point: Of all the things that kids know how to do, they know how to say what they think, tell you how they feel, and they are not afraid to ask for what they want. They are unafraid of how they sound, and not worried if they are getting it right. Just honest words of desire. This is how Jesus is inviting us to step into prayer— honest and authentic.

Not long ago I pulled out old VHS tapes from when my children were young. I sat down with Mary Anne to remember and find delight in our shared memories. There was one tape that showed our two daughters (Katie and Annie) on Santa's knee. Katie was probably 5 and Annie 3. My beautiful daughters were bright-eyed with wonder. Santa was a very kind older gentleman— exactly what you'd expect from the role. My daughters sat quietly, one on each of his knees. Then Santa asked, "What do you want Santa to bring for you this Christmas?"

Then my youngest daughter Annie sprang into action. Finding her voice, undaunted by this strange man dressed in red, she piped up.

"I . . . I . . . I want Puppy Surprise!"

Santa repeated and asked,

"Annie wants Puppy Surprise. What about Katie?"

Before Katie could even find a word, Annie burst forth again and pointed toward her sister. "She wants Baby All Gone!"

Katie just smiled and nodded her head in the affirmative. The cuteness factor was unbearable. Any father would have wanted to buy every Puppy Surprise in the toy department! What I loved was that shameless authenticity. The absence of the self-editing that is so common to us all. Just knowing what she wanted and saying so. It was compelling.

God already knows what I'm are not telling him. I need to say it more than he needs to hear it. I are not informing him. I am finding the humility and the honesty to admit what's true. When I come to God like this, magic happens. In that moment I am helped not because I said my prayers right, but because I said them honestly. As it turns out, prayer (like all good relationships) cannot bear up under the weight of pretending. I must learn how to say what I think, learn to honestly process how I feel, and say exactly what I want. Why? Because as it turns out, God likes authenticity. Who doesn't?

Why is it so hard to be straight-forward with God? Probably because it is hard to be that way with myself. I have a long history of hiding. I've perfected the art of avoiding myself. I begin prayer by thinking I'm going to inform God. Meanwhile, he is using prayer to bring me face-to-face with myself. He makes much of me and is unwilling to move forward while I'm hiding or pretending. I have found him to be extremely patient but unwilling to budge on this point. If I want candor WITH him, then I must bring candor TO him.Perhaps you feel that it is the candor of God that you are trying to avoid? You have him pictured as the one who smites those who do wrong? Nobody feels safe enough with THAT God to say it as it is. But that picture of God is incomplete.

Again, another story from Lewis' *Chronicles of Narnia*. In *The Silver Chair,* there is a scene where the two children, Jill and Eustace, have magically found themselves displaced from England and located in the world of Narnia. When they arrive in this world, they find themselves close to the edge of a ridiculously high cliff— so high that only clouds can be seen. Jill ventures too close to the edge, and Eustace, feeling like she is being careless, reaches out for her to draw her back. She is frustrated by his interference and as she yanks her arm out of his reach, Eustace stumbles and falls over the edge himself. At this moment, a lion runs from the forest and blows a powerful wind of breath towards where Eustace is falling. This, of course, is Aslan, The Lion, bringing Eustace to safety. When he was finished blowing his breath toward the fallen

Eustace, "Without a glance to Jill the Lion rose to its feet . . . stalked slowly away, back into the forest."

The next scene captures God's unrelenting demand that we face ourselves honestly. As Jill begins to make her way through the forest, she hears the sound of water. She draws nearer to the sound and her thirst increases. The more she seeks the water, the thirstier she becomes. Just as she feels that she will die from thirst, she finds the stream of water. But finding the stream, she freezes in her tracks. Between her and the stream is the Lion.

> "Are you not thirsty?" said the Lion. "I am dying of thirst," said Jill. "Then drink," said the Lion. "May I— could I— would you mind going away while I do?" said Jill. The Lion answered this only by a look and a very low growl. And as Jill gazed at its motionless bulk, she realized that she might as well have asked the whole mountain to move aside for her convenience. The delicious rippling noise of the stream was driving her nearly frantic. "Will you promise not to — do anything to me, if I do come?" said Jill. "I make no promise," said the Lion. Jill was so thirsty now that, without noticing it, she had come a step nearer. Do you eat girls?" she said. "I have swallowed up girls and boys, women and men, kings and emperors, cities and realms," said the Lion. It didn't say this as if it were boasting, nor as if it were sorry, nor as if it were angry. It just said it. "I daren't come and drink," said Jill. "Then you will die of thirst," said the Lion. "Oh dear!" said Jill, coming another step nearer. "I suppose I must go and look

for another stream then." There is no other stream," said the Lion. It never occurred to Jill to disbelieve the Lion – no one who had seen his stern face could do that – and her mind suddenly made itself up. It was the worst thing she had ever had to do, but she went forward to the stream, knelt down, and began scooping up water in her hand. It was the coldest, most refreshing water she had ever tasted. You didn't need to drink much of it, for it quenched your thirst at once.

"Come here," said the Lion. And she had to. She was almost between its front paws now, looking straight into its face. But she couldn't stand that for long; she dropped her eyes. "Human Child," said the Lion, "Where is the Boy?" "He fell over the cliff," said Jill, and added, "Sir." She didn't know what else to call him, and it sounded cheek to call him nothing. "How did he come to do that, Human Child?" "He was trying to stop me from falling, Sir." "Why were you so near the edge, Human Child?" "I was showing off, Sir?" "That is a very good answer, Human Child. Do so no more and now" (here for the first time the Lion's face became a little less stern). "The boy is safe."[14]

Whether I have wrongs that I need to admit, or desires unmet that I need to say, or realities of my life that are crushing me, whatever the case may be, God waits patiently for honest words. When they are given the atmosphere of the conversation transforms. Just like in marriage, friendship, or even business— gut level honesty always changes the conversation. In prayer, God sits between my current state and the breakthrough that I desperately long to see and leads me to face myself.

This should surprise no one. We all like honesty in our conversations. In a real relationship it is the only way forward.

Stay in the Present Tense

My favorite moment is Now. It is the only time arranged by God for me to know him. In fact, all relationships are made for the present tense. The only place where vital relational connection can be made is in the moment we call now. The moment I stop opening up in the present tense, the relationship shifts. It goes into the past tense. Which means I can be grateful for the history, but I cannot love. Like God, love is perpetually and eternally in the present tense.

He is a dwelling God. He is not a distant cosmic force as some would refer to the "universe", nor is he pantheistical (dwelling in everything at the same time). He is God, dwelling where he chooses and (because he is well-mannered) where he is invited. His invitation to us is a clear "if, then" proposal. We are invited to relationally abide in him, and he promises that he will then abide in us. The New Testament word for abide means to stay present. God is inviting us to stay in the present tense with him. Those who do so carry something way more potent than those who just know what they believe. The difference is likened to someone who believes in cars. They can tell us what it is supposed to be like. But someone who pulls up in a car can demonstrate its reality by offering you a ride.

If you ever wonder where God is— first look at your calendar, then your clock, then at the ground beneath your feet and understand that he is right here, right now.

A few years ago, I was listening to an interview with a worship songwriter who was touring across the states. The reporter asked him, "What has been your favorite moment of the tour so far?" He answered, "My favorite moment is always now because that is the moment when God is available to me." The elegant simplicity of the thought inspired me. It was not new information for me nor is it for you. It just reminded me of something critical that I'd forgotten to remember.

You see, sometimes important truths that can change your life are like a picture that you hung in your hallway last year. It's always there and you've walked by it dozens of times. But because it is so ordinary to your hallway walk, you forget to notice it. It hangs there in the hallway, as beautiful as ever, but its beauty is of no use to you. Even though it is hanging in plain view you've effectively forgotten about it. Likewise, some truths are so true and universally accepted that they stop being noticed. If we fail to notice, then we fail to harness the power. **What**

good is it for me to believe that God is available to me in every moment If I've stopped looking for him in the present tense?

If I want to talk to God, I don't have to wait till tomorrow. I don't have to get in my car and drive across town. God is always in the present tense. Do not dismiss this as a trite saying. It is, in fact, powerful information telling you and me where you can find God. Right here, right now. When you begin to reckon upon the power of this truth then you will stop deferring to the future and reminiscing about the past. You will wake up to the fact that the Kingdom of Heaven is like a door in the floor under your feet, always there. Like every normal door, it must be opened. You have to show up and open up to God's presence. That can only be done in the present moment.

Marked by His Presence

The experience of God's presence has ruined me. I can't settle for pretend substitutes. I have tasted and seen his goodness. I have entered into the bonfire of his glory. Warmed by the glow of his abiding. I've heard his instructions, like a lantern in my soul, sometimes a whisper, just the size of a candle. It is an abiding that testifies that he is with me. A burning that keeps me coming back for more.

If you feel discouraged because your prayers yield nothing that resembles these expectations, you are reading the right book. Continue reading. Remember in the movie *Hook* it took Peter Banning, the lawyer, longer than he expected to become Peter Pan again. With much pain, trial and error, and a large dose of unbelief he arrived at his moment of awakening. Until that moment, it all seemed like fantasy, a pack of lies, delusions pushed forward by misfits who have nowhere else to belong. But like Peter Banning, you are only one thin moment away from an encounter from which you will never recover. Like him— you may soon be flying.

Invocation

Next Step:
Look for an awareness of God's presence in prayer.

Scripture:
"I will not leave you as orphans; I will come to you. . . On that day you will realize that I am in my Father, and you are in me, and I am in you." (John 14:18+20, NIV)

Quote:
*"The witness of God is his presence." **Pastor Kevin Queen** (Crosspoint Church, Nashville)*

Prayer:

Holy Son of God, help me not to miss the point. As I resolve to show up, teach me to step into your presence. I've known loneliness, now I want to know you. Help me to expect you and seek you with an open heart. Teach me how to treasure the present tense and come like a child, armed with honesty. You have known me, let me now know you. Not by what I've been told but by my own relational experience with you.

Section Two: Stay

THE REASON WE'RE ALL IMPRESSED

Starting is easier than staying. Staying is work. It takes resolve and deliberate attention. Prayer is the same. Just like our earthly relationships, there are additional skills required to abide in a long-term relationship. Starting must mature into staying. Beginning prayer must mature into abiding prayer.

Chapter 3
PROTECT MOMENTUM

Make good trades

Motivation comes from experience. If the relationship doesn't pay off in desirable experiences, then we drift. We get distracted. We opt for "better use" of our time.

Prayer must turn your access to God into experiences with God. Without the payoff of experiences, prayer turns into hours of uninspired religious duty. Prayer cannot be the "community service" verdict of a God in a bad mood. It must be the invitation to make the acquaintance with the one who made chocolate cake possible. The one who first imagined the face of a baboon. The one who knew what Bach would sound like before the first song was written. The God of mathematics, intricate systems that work perfectly. The keeper of the secrets of quantum mechanics, and the artist who thought of every color in the crayon box. The One who knows the answer to questions that we are not smart enough to even ask. He created the inescapable pull of morality. He imagined the paralyzing beauty of the human voice. Wind across vocal cords making sounds so beautiful it hurts. The God who imagined love and invited you to participate in its heights and its painful depths. He counted the addition of sex as a worthwhile complement to the human experience. So many surprises and delights hidden for us to find.

But in prayer God invites us to himself. The Originator, the Creator, the good Father. What makes this invitation more than just words on paper? It must be an experience. **The motivation for continued prayer comes from the experience of the relationship inside of prayer – it's a sacred cycle.** "Should" and "Ought" attached to prayer will never yield lasting momentum. We must mature to higher tutors than obligation. In Psalm 38 the scriptures give us a clue:
"Taste and see that the Lord is good."

He didn't send an excel spreadsheet with instructions for logging our prayer minutes. He didn't place a heavy mandate with a daily minimal requirement. He invited us to something more like being called to the dinner table. When you are hungry, food is never boring.

Most evenings, Mary Anne and I eat at home and enjoy her delicious cooking. Our garden has produced well this year, so the food is homegrown and fresh. By the time we get to this part of our day, we are both sufficiently hungry and excited. It's a curated experience of well-prepared food and joyful engagement, topped off with coffee and a small dish of peaches and cream. A 5-star experience. By the time we are through, we are satisfied and happy.

When the scriptures invite us to "Taste and see," it's like the Lord pointing to your favorite dining experience and saying, "Like that! Come to me like that!" Like the much-anticipated call of "Dinner's ready!" to the hungry person, God calls to us. But we must taste. To not taste is to miss at least half of the point.

Some who call themselves "teachers of the Word" dull the expectations of the church when they proclaim that faith alone with no experience is normal. They transpose the invitation from "Taste and See" to "Trust and Wait." Trust and wait are perfectly true postures of prayer, but they are not an end in themselves. They are not the destination; they are campsites on the way to the destination. Relationships do not survive in a perpetual trust and wait mode.

"It is a solemn thing, and no small scandal in the Kingdom, to see God's children starving while actually seated at the Father's table."[15] A.W. Tozer

"Taste" is more than an invitation to show up and step into his presence. It is the open-door invitation to **experience God himself.** Just as the call to dinner is likely to make my mouth water, so the invitation to prayer should be properly anticipated with the expectation of fellowship with him. But it's not only "taste," it's also "see."

I love that Jesus carried demonstrations of power. He taught with authority, he healed in miraculous power, he threw out dark spirits with a word, he announced something to believe, but then backed it up with the power of an experience. In prayer he invites us to draw near in faith but then follows up on the invitation by allowing us to see the benefits of his presence.

We are sometimes tempted to think God has changed— that somewhere along the line he disengaged and that he no longer demonstrates his presence with the power and the authority of results we can see. We are tempted to ration down our expectations; mold our beliefs down to the size of our weak encounters. The opposite is recommended. Raise your expectations up to the size of God's invitation. Whatever you choose to believe in prayer is what you are likely to see. And then, predictably, what you taste and see will become the motivating current that brings you back to him over and over.

My friend Pastor Jason Berry relayed to me a personal story about the kind of impression a proper dining encounter can leave. Jason said that the previous summer he'd gone to visit his brother over the July 4th holiday. His brother had slow cooked 'pig butt' (a cut commonly known as Boston Butt which comes from the shoulder region; Jason was caught up in his story, I wasn't going to correct him). His brother bragged to Jason that it was going to "change his life." He took it as normal exaggeration but when he arrived at his brother's house and partook, he almost teared up as he remembered. "It was the best thing I'd ever tasted!"

Now, one year later, he admitted, the meal was so unforgettable that he'd thought about it constantly ever since. It was so surprisingly good. He's living in anticipation of returning to his brother's house this year, and he's already put in a meal request for 'pig butt.'

The experience of spiritual closeness with God marks me and motivates me to keep coming back. Some moments intense with holiness, other days slight like a whisper. But ripe with the ability to keep me coming back.

Momentum

In 2004 the Boston Red Sox faced the New York Yankees in the American League Championship Series. Though the Red Sox had finished three games behind the Yankees in the regular season, the Sox made it into the postseason as the Wild Card team. They quickly dropped the first three games of a best of seven series to the Yankees. They were down three and needed to win four in a row – something no other team in MLB history had ever done.

I'm sure most of the Red Sox team had begun the descent into resignation— the harsh reality that they were almost certainly going to lose the series. In a counterculture move of undaunted optimism, Kevin Millar walked around to his Red Sox teammates during pre-game batting practice. He scoffed at the notion that they might lose and began fill up his teammate's ears (as if he was addressing the whole Yankee team),

"Don't let the Sox win tonight!"[16] Then he would outline for them the certain path of Red Sox victory if they could just win the game that night.

What was he doing? Working on momentum. He'd been in sports long enough to know the mysterious power of it. Those who have it are almost undefeatable. When you lose it, the game can't end quickly enough. Millar knew the Sox needed all the help that could be mustered.

The Red Sox were down by one run in the bottom of the ninth, facing Mariano Rivera (the closer for the Yanks). As the clock drew near to midnight, Kevin Millar came to the plate. He drew a walk on four straight pitches – what?! Dave Roberts came in to pinch run. He got a huge lead and drew three throws over to first. On the first pitch to the plate, he stole second base.

One run down, bottom of the ninth. Bill Miller was the batter at the plate. Man on second, nobody out: Fenway Park was on fire with possibility. On the third pitch he sent a single up the middle and Dave Roberts scored to tie the game and send it into extra innings. The Red Sox went on to win on a walk-off homer in the twelfth. Momentum jumped in their corner, and they never looked back. They came back to defeat the Yankees in seven. They advanced to the World Series and beat the St. Louis Cardinals in four straight games. That's momentum.

How does this relate to prayer?

Accumulated experiences with God create spiritual momentum.

The physical force of momentum has an equation: **P = M x V**

In the physical universe, the momentum of an object is equal to the mass of the object (M) times the velocity of the object (V). In other words, if it's big and it's moving fast, it has momentum. As is often the case, things in the physical universe show us how things in the spiritual universe work.

Metaphorically speaking, God is the ultimate in spiritual mass. He is infinite in discovery. I could never exhaust the experience of who He is. The more I "taste" and "see" of him, the bigger he becomes in my life story. The bigger he becomes in my personal experience, the more momentum I gain. I can think of velocity in the spiritual realm not in terms of speed, but as depth and consistency of my fellowship with God.

Personal discovery of God x the depth and consistency of that discovery = spiritual momentum.

Just like in the realm of sports, spiritual momentum creates a trajectory of wins. Life wins.Breakthrough in life. Not the elimination of struggle or pain but sufficient mass and velocity to break through to the other side. Even though there is a challenge, I have joined the winning team. The King of Kings, the Lord of Lords, The First and the Last, The Beginning and the End, the One of whom scripture triumphantly declares: "Of the increase of his government there will be no end." (Isaiah 9:7, ESV) I have stepped into a spiritual current that is eternally increasing.

But like the requirement of excellence in sports, the glory of momentum is preceded by a commitment to the everyday fundamentals. Championship caliber teams are not created overnight, neither is prayer momentum. In fact, the predictable arc of all relationships is the tendency to take the relationship for granted. Forgetting the importance of the everyday fundamentals, it's the storyline of a hundred movies and a thousand failed marriages. Take my eye off the prized possession of shared closeness and the relationship that was once my most prized possession will get lost in the foggy haze of self-orientation. Prayer is subject to this same kind of loss. When momentum diminishes, the felt enjoyment slowly drains. Something vital and very dear is being lost. There are key battlegrounds where I must keep watch.

Making Trades

Relationships are built on the foundation of important battle grounds where trades are decided and protected. What is a trade? It's a common life maneuver where I say yes to one thing and no to everything else. I trade one thing of lesser value to get something of greater value. It's the very essence of a wedding ceremony. When I chose my wife, I un-chose every other option. I traded the untethered freedom of living alone for the holy collaboration of marriage. Having chosen her, I am now building a life with her on the back of numerous other trades.

I say yes to important things that help the relationship flourish. But notice, almost every yes requires a reciprocal no to other things. This dynamic is fully in play in our desire to build a life of knowing God. There are battlegrounds that demand my vigilance. Making trades is not a "one and done" endeavor; it is an ongoing turf war. Not me battling God over turf, but me battling myself to keep the right trades in play for the good of my relationship with God.

Trading the Right to Rule (Joining Jesus)

This is trade number one. "Jesus is Lord" is more than an ancient phrase; it's a life declaration about who is in charge. Momentum with God will accrue life wins but let me be super clear about how those wins are defined. I am not inviting Jesus to join me; I am joining him. He is not my co-pilot. He is my King and I daily trade in all the delusion of self-governing for the reward of his benevolent conquest inside of me.

Joining Jesus is active and continuous. I choose him, and I continue to allow this choice to become the defining decision of my whole life. When I am clear about this, the atmosphere of my soul is ripe for momentum with God. When I am not, the haze of self-orientation eventually rolls back in like a fog, and momentum pauses. When that happens, it's time to re-up on this fundamental trade. I have to reorient myself to take a stance that is like the apostle Paul who declared over his own life:

> *"I consider everything as loss because of the surpassing worth of knowing Christ Jesus my Lord. For his sake I have suffered the loss of all things and count them as rubbish, in order that I may gain Christ and be found in him . . ."(Philippians 3:8+9, ESV)*

This language sounds grandiose, but I've learned this trade plays out subtly. It warrants my attention every day. It's the answer to the simple question— who is in charge today? Not the memorized answer. Not the one required by my identity as a Christian. But the honest answer at the center of a wrestling match where I must yield.

Trade Time

Time is the next thing we all trade when we decide to build a relationship. It's the taken-for-granted thing that, when neglected, gets us in trouble fast. When I become careless with my time, I become careless with the relationship. Since prayer is the fundamental way in which I build a relationship with God, I must keep an eye on how I use my time and how much of it I protect for connecting with God. The emphasis here is not how much time, but the protection of dedicated time.

I realize that costly investments of time can easily look like a "works' based system where we feel as if we are gaining points with God by how much sacrifice we can muster. This approach doesn't work, and it misses the point. Love is always measured by its cost, its sacrifice, its investment. But if the motive becomes a payback system of sacrifice, then love is not in play. Love chases because it loves, not to be paid back. Costly sacrifice, when offered freely as a gift, turns into an accrual of intimacy. The investment of time proves the chase of love.

Tozer says it well,

"No shortcut exist. God has not bowed to our nervous haste nor embraced the methods of our machine age. It is well that we accept the hard truth now: the Man who would know God must give time to Him. He must count no time wasted which is spent in the cultivation of his acquaintance."[17]

But understand that in this last line where he says "the cultivation of His acquaintance", the guarantee of experience is encoded. For how else Dows one become acquainted with another, except by the experience of being with them?

Trade Amusement for Abiding

We all learn early in life to cover up our spiritual hunger with as many distractions as we can invent. We medicate with diversions. We amuse ourselves into a stupor, opting for anything that entertains until sleep comes back around. I'm not advocating for the eradication of fun. I'm pointing out that we seek out distraction through entertainment that camouflages our need. Social Media, On-Demand TV, 24-hour options in sports, hobbies, church activities, kid's sports and personal development – all good in moderation. But nothing is good that crowds out my ability for abiding honesty with God. Prayer interrupts the self-medicating amusement cycle. It requires me to face myself and then bring myself into his presence to learn how to abide with him.

Trade Resignation for Possibility

Resignation is a prayer buster.

Proverbs 13:12 warns us, '**Hope deferred makes the heart sick.**"

This is the experience of resignation so common to humanity. Life trains us to put hope at a distance. Seasons of pain have reduced us to shadow versions of ourselves. Like a cold glass of water to the face, disappointment has stolen our belief in the future, and we embrace resignation. We trade in our desire to fight for what we want. We trim down our hopes to what we think is achievable. We become resigned to a lesser life because a life with less aspiration is more emotionally manageable. However, the temptation to defer hope is from the darker management team on the planet. We must actively resist.

The Kingdom of heaven forcefully assaults resignation with possibility. You must finish the verse: **"Hope deferred makes the heart sick but a desire fulfilled is a tree of life."**(Proverbs 13:12, ESV)

Prayer is the path to desire realized. It is for confronting resignation. It is for breaking out of smaller ceilings closing in to smother your life. Desire exists for further discovery. It is the breadcrumb path towards your unique calling under God's leadership.Everybody hurts. Everybody suffers. Everybody has unmet expectations. However resignation doesn't happen to you, it is a chosen posture. It shifts the gears of your life into passive neutral. But your relationship with God is made for forward movement. Stewarding your momentum with him requires you to resist the gravity of resignation.

Trade Maybe for a Whole-Hearted Yes

God protects your right to choose him. You can say yes to his invitation, or you can say no. This is the way it must be. Only love willfully given is truly love. Your yes is not a one-time occurrence, it is an everyday choice.

Over time, however, your yes can degrade into a no. Most of the time this is not because you changed your mind, it's because you lost momentum. You lost forward action. You lost your whole-hearted response. **Your no is often not an overt no, it's your inability to sustain a yes.** However, no is a complete sentence. It doesn't matter how you got there. Consequences will follow.

And "Maybe" is equally no good. A partial yes is a no. Heaven has a particular distaste for lukewarm. God is pure forward momentum, wholehearted and without any hesitation towards you. Anything less than a wholehearted yes toward him will drain the momentum of your relationship with him. So, keep a watchful eye over your heart as Proverbs has prescribed, ***"Watch over your heart with all diligence."*** *(Proverbs 4:23, NASB)*

Prayer without heart turns into legalism. If you ever find yourself feeling resentful toward God, this is one of the places to look. Legalism tries to storm the gates of heaven with human effort carrying a basket of "Should and Ought to." You will find the gates will not open. Though you bleed hours of sacrifice, the heavens remain closed. The gospel is for your brokenness, your deep hunger and spiritual thirst. When you come to the gates of prayer with these in hand, you will find that the doors were never closed. The veil that keeps you from God has been torn in two by the very hand of heaven. The only one who can keep you out is you.

Keep a weather-eye on your heart's disposition. An active Yes cannot be assumed; it must be given each day.

Trade Instant Gratification for Building History with God
When I give God the treasure of my time, He becomes my treasure.[18]

One ordinary day about seven years ago, I was ascending the stairs to one of my customary prayer rooms. I had my iPhone on shuffle as I walked along. A song began. I sensed the Lord. It was intimate . . . close. He was telling me something about the investment of my time with him over the years. The song was *The Book of Love*, Peter Gabriel's version. The song is a metaphor that captures the highs and lows, the magic and the absurdities of the experience of love by making it analogous to a book. The first line caught my attention:

"The book of love is long and boring."

As I ambled along toward a private place to be with God, it was as if he began to speak to me through the song. He was affirming that love builds undefeatable bonds through the *long and boring*. My heart was captivated by this moment where my Creator was telling me how much he valued my company. He was acknowledging that sometimes love is *long and boring* but that is what proves its mettle. In the long lines of daily dwelling with him, something undeniable was being forged. Nobody can take back those hours. They are given in honest desire and offered freely. The mundane minutes invested in the direction of the one who is loved turns to magic.

To this day, the haunting melody from that song will make me weep. He loves me and we've built something that no one can steal. It's the strand of a thousand shared minutes stacked up in proof of a life together. Moments kept, memories cataloged, time given. The unmistakable mark of familiarity is earned. It is accrued in the currency of time invested but also in the repeated opening of one's heart.

One year ago today, I attended a funeral of a friend of mine. He died in a tragic car accident at a very early age. His life-long best friend stood to speak. I was drawn into their relationship as he shared one story after another. His affection was validated by the stories. Everyone felt comfortable to laugh at the gentle ease of their comradery— a hundred shared tales of life experience that would be impossible to contrive, forged in the crucible of real minutes of real days. Friendship given; friendship returned. A similar mark should be branded upon my life with God. A trained softening of the will and a sustained open heart. Like friendship. The hours traded build history and an undefeatable bond.

Trade Shallow Living for Sacred Purpose

Prayer is the sign-up sheet for the life-purpose for which I was created. Something to get me up in the morning, a way to guide my life's decisions, a code that influences my behavior and shapes my goals, a way to have a sense of direction and draw contentment. The absence of purpose is a breeding ground for shallow living— a slippery slope into a nightmarish existence.

God alone is the source of meaning that extends beyond mere utility. Reality shapes around His nature. No matter how many mental constructs may be contrived by an unbelieving world, we can't escape the need that we have for him. Do not skim here. God is holy, virtuous, and eternal. To be anchored in Him is to have hope. To slip from his company is to wander into enemy waters —the dark regions that hint at the true nature of hell. Anyone who has ever lived in a season of hopelessness knows how desperately dark it is when life's meaning begins to cascade downward. We slip slightly at first, but if not arrested through a return to God, what started as a subtle slip of the snow turns into a dark avalanche.

In John Milton's *Paradise Lost*, Satan self-assesses his separation from God and absence of sacred meaning when he says:

> "Me miserable! Which way shall I fly infinite wrath and infinite despair? Which way I fly is hell; myself am hell; And in the lowest deep a lower deep, still threatening to devour me, opens wide."[19]

Contrasted to this are the words of Jesus who took the time to instill hope in the heart of the woman at the well in John 4.

Jesus said to her, "If you knew the gift of God and who it is that asks you for a drink, you would have asked him, and he would have given you living water." The women replied, "Sir, you have nothing to draw with and the well is deep. Where can you get this living water? Are you greater than our father Jacob, who gave us the well and drank from it himself?" He responded, "Everyone who drinks this water will be thirsty again, but whoever drinks the water I give them will never thirst. Indeed, the water I give them will become in them a spring of water welling up to eternal life." Her reply opens up heaven's sacred purpose for her life, "Sir, give me this water" [20]

Jesus draws her in. He brings her to a heavenly Father who holds the patent on satisfaction. He is eternally satisfied. Internally sourced and happy without condition. The soul who apprehends him in prayer finds himself lassoed into happiness in its rawest form. Wellbeing unending. From that sacred place we are postured for earthly accomplishment robust with purpose. Slowly and over time, we find our unique purpose holding God's leading hand.

Experiences follow

Spiritual experiences are the result of making the right relational trades. Time invested, turning from endless distraction, wholeheartedly setting my course to build history with God, they become a way of life. Trades are choices that become habits. That is not to say that making the right trades becomes easier, but they do become more entrenched in my way of life. The successful pilgrim realizes that momentum is a life-long endeavor and builds a pursuit of God that is made for distance [more on that later].

Delight: The Last word on keeping momentum.

This chapter has made much of human effort and doing the right things to stay motivated. The final word must be that God himself is chasing us. As Tozer says, "God is always previous."[181] Before we chase God, we can draw strength from the knowledge that God is chasing us.

Though "trades" can begin to sound like arduous climbing, the true dynamic is one of delight. We build a life that is designed for daily delight in the Lord. Remembering who he is, celebrating what he has done, imagining what is yet to come. Building a life designed to step into his momentum. He is pure delight. Undefeated victory. He is playing chase too.

Invocation

Next Step:
Pay attention to the trades in your life and use them to cultivate experiences with God.

Scripture:
"Taste and see that the Lord is good; blessed is the one who takes refuge in him."
Psalm 34:8

Quotes:
Winning is not a sometime thing; it's an all-time thing. You don't win once in a while; you don't do things right once in a while; you do them right all of the time. Winning is a habit. Unfortunately, so is losing. (Vince Lombardi)

Prayer:

Father, I come to you with a head full of beliefs about you, but I want to know you by experience. I want to learn your presence and sense you in the room with me. I ask that you awaken me. Open my inward ears that I may know your voice, that I may be marked and motivated to return over and over. I'm not asking for proof; I just want to be where you are. Help me build a life and make the right trades so that I may draw near to you.

Chapter 4
Start Listening

Surprised in Sunday School

I grew up going to church. Southern Baptist was my particular variety of upbringing. It was a perfectly traditional affair, and by traditional I don't mean misguided or clueless. It was reminiscent of a brand of church that is fading fast in the American landscape. It was a community of humble believers in Jesus whose primary expression of their faith was to attend church on Sunday morning, Sunday night and then again on Wednesday. It was the gathering of neighbors meeting underneath a steeple. It was stained glass, an organ, and a piano. It smelled of dark wood, smooth pews, and potluck suppers. The sounds were chatty conversations and hymns being sung, a perfectly safe place to grow up. I loved this church.

I grew up with these people. I knew them and they knew me. It was earthy and wonderful. Good people being good-hard working, moral people doing life together.However, rare were the moments when I intersected something that felt sacred. You could argue that good people in community around their faith is sacred— I would agree. But my heart was looking for something to show me that God was there. Not theoretically, but actually there, in person. Not just a creed to memorize, but a supernatural being to charge the atmosphere.

Sunday school refers to age-appropriate classes where we listened to volunteers try to teach something meaningful from the scriptures. They did this primarily through reading from a little lesson plan book called, 'The Baptist Quarterly'. These little books had ready-made lessons mapped out for the volunteers to teach their class.

Let me just say what many of us with similar experience and personality already know: Sunday School could be miserable business. It reminds me of how Mark Twain's no-nonsense character Huckleberry Finn described sitting under the tutelage of Miss Watson:

"Then for an hour it was deadly dull and I was all fidgety ... Then she told me about the bad place and I said I wished I was there. She got mad, then, but I didn't mean no harm. All I wanted was to go somewheres; all I wanted was a change, I warn't particular."[21]

You get the picture.But as often happens with God, I got a surprise one Sunday.

I was about eight years old, and my teacher was a kind lady named Mrs. Beck. Mrs. Beck all the sudden took a hushed tone and began to relay an experience that she'd had with God. My fidgeting calmed, and my eyes widened as I heard for the first time in my life someone claim that God had spoken to them.

She said that she had been in her house when God had spoken the simple sentence, "Sue, I need you." I'd been in church my whole life and never heard anyone claim to have heard God speak. And it wasn't just her story that seemed incredible, it was her demeanor as well— her whole countenance changed. She was calm but deeply resolute about her experience.

I was normally a rowdy distraction to the class but now I was captured with wonder.

"Did you actually hear his voice?" I asked.

She looked me square in the eyes, "Yes".

I'm sure I followed up with questions like: "What did he sound like?" "Did you see anything?" But I was marked. My young mind reasoned, "If God still speaks to people, then I want to hear him too."

Prayer is for hearing God speak

Relationships are two-way. Both sides must contribute, or it is not a relationship. This is where many of us tap out. We've spoken to heaven and heard nothing back. We've taken the stance that says, "If God does speak, I would've heard something by now." So, we shut down our hearts. We pack up our prayer suitcase and head for the hills called 'no response.'

However, what we don't admit is that we often treat God more like a customer service desk than a relationship. We do business with him only when we want something. We put high expectations on him to perform according to our need and become offended when things don't go the way we want. Then we write a bad review and bury it in our soul.

Learning to hear God speak is like learning someone's personality. It takes time, investment, proper motive, and repeated experience. It begins with the belief that he will speak. The person who carries such a belief will get alone and draw near to God (preferably with an open Bible). They will wait and listen. They will approach in an attitude of worship. This person draws near to know, not to drop off a wish list.

The scriptures do not stutter in the belief that God speaks. *"In the beginning was the Word, and the Word was with God, and the Word was God".* (John 1:1) *He* defines himself as the Word. It is in his nature to speak. A.W. Tozer says it this way:

"A word is a medium by which thoughts are expressed, and the application of the term to the Eternal Son (Jesus) leads us to believe that self-expression is inherent in the Godhead, that God is forever seeking to speak Himself out to His creation. The whole Bible supports the idea. God is speaking. Not God spoke, but God is speaking. He is by His nature continuously articulate."[22]

When someone claims to have "heard God speak," it is usually treated with either intrigue or disdain, depending on the audience. It is often viewed as odd— the exception, not the rule.

I remember watching a video from one of the major news outlets. The video was a rant by one of the hosts of a show called "The View." She was responding to a political figure who'd declared publicly that Jesus speaks to him. What got me was the dichotomy of her perspective. She wasn't an atheist or even agnostic. She made sure to categorize herself as Christian. But her critique went like this:

"It's one thing to talk to Jesus, it's another thing when Jesus talks to you." (Her tone clearly in the camp of *"are you kidding me?"*) The audience in hearty agreement clapped. Then she added, "That's called mental illness"

I smiled a conflicted smile. She calls herself Christian, and yet, her point of view opposes and makes absurd what the scriptures teach us to expect. The other part of me, though, held compassion. I know how we end up resigned like her. When the silence of God is normal, then the voice of God seems so radical as to be an illness.

Again, Tozer helps us here:

> "We talk of him much and loudly, but we secretly think of him as being absent... We are lonely with an ancient and cosmic loneliness. We are each like a little child lost in a crowded market who has strayed but a few feet from its mother, yet because she cannot be seen, the child is inconsolable. So we try by every method devised by religion to relieve our fears and heal our hidden sadness; but with all our efforts we remain unhappy still, with the settled

despair of men alone in a vast and deserted universe. **But for all our fears we are not alone. Our trouble is that we think of ourselves as being alone.**"[23]

Most of us carry a worldview that would allow the possibility of a present tense, speaking God. But the pursuit of prayer requires us to move from possibility to **expectation.** Worldview holds the core of our beliefs, but our mindset molds our expectations. Many of us believe in God but have no expectation that flows from that belief. Worldview beliefs may comfort us when life feels stormy, but it can't actually calm the storm. The trouble is that we've been slowly swayed from our supernatural origins. A thousand interactions that are hopelessly human have surreptitiously shaped our perspective away from its "made in the image of God" birth rite. As Mark Sayers says in his book <u>Reappearing Church</u>, "Christians have internalized the secular map of reality."[24]

This map has invaded our perspective and the experiences of our lives follow suit. As we think in our hearts, so we become. Our anemic view of God then seems to validate our secular assumptions. But God is not at fault, we sabotage ourselves. We've partaken deeply of the Kool-aid; the tastemakers of our culture have told us what is real. God has been pushed to the outer rim if not uninvited altogether. If we think of God as distant and silent, then prayer is a fool's errand. But the scriptures say something different.

Scripture outlines the mindset of a listening life. It starts with uncomplicated faith. The belief that not only does God exist but that he is a rewarder of those who seek him (Hebrews 11:6). This simple mindset turns the silent complexity of an unyielding sky into a heaven with access. From this vantage point, prayer is a doorway to a present God. The scriptures lead us from story to story of men and women in actual encounters with a real person. They prayed— they spoke to God and heard him speak back.

We'd like to know how we can be more like the ones we read about in scripture— building a life that is designed for hearing. Like a table set for fine dining, everything intentionally put in place— we need a life for hearing and following God's voice.

The disciple Thomas admitted his confusion to Jesus, even as he reclined with him at the table. In John 14 he says, "Lord, we don't know where you are going, so how can we know the way?" Jesus gave a famous answer that I will use as an outline for setting the table of God's voice:

"I am the way and the truth and the life." (John 14:6, NIV)

He gave us a pattern for prayer. He gave us the scriptures. And he sent the Holy Spirit.

All conspire together to lead us to his voice.

The Way: The Pattern for listening

At the beginning of his public ministry Jesus taught the crowds foundational principles of how God's Kingdom works. This is a portion of scripture we call the Sermon on the Mount (Matthew 5 through 7).

Included in this teaching is a pattern that Jesus recommended for prayer. It includes the Lord's Prayer (more on that in the next chapter), but before he gives the Lord's Prayer, he says,

"When you pray, go into your room, and shut the door and pray to your Father who is in secret. And your Father who sees in secret will reward you." (Matthew 6:6, ESV)

Included here is a simple pattern for building a prayer movement ready to hear God speak.

Show up: *When you pray*

Jesus doesn't speak about prayer as if it is one of many options. No, he speaks about it as if it is an assumed part of your life. Rightly so. As we've already said, I cannot have a relationship with anyone without talking to them. We talked about this in chapter one, but here again is another reminder that the invitation to pray is an invitation to pause your life and show up. Prayer is for the experience of hearing from God, but it begins with showing up— your presence standing before him.

Protect Privacy: *When you pray, go into your room.*

When I was a young boy, I attended my father's basketball games. He was the high school coach, and the games were a magical playground for me. The teams he coached were known for their defense and for winning games they were supposed to lose. Because his teams were winners, the gym was always packed on game nights. The stands jammed with people, loud and proud of their team.

One of my favorite moments was half-time. Because I was the coach's son, I had access to the locker room at half-time. My dad's half-time speeches were a work of art. I was proud of him. But I remember the feeling of being allowed into the inner sanctum. This was protected and private space where only those who paid the price to be on the team were allowed in. The gym may have been packed outside but only the chosen few could be in the locker room.

Jesus is outlining the path of prayer the same way – private and protected. Strong relationships always protect privacy. They are exclusive— no one else is allowed in.

The priority of the relationship is proven through the private nature of its interactions. Whether it's your best friend, your spouse, or a teammate, when privacy is protected there is a personal currency in the relationship. Shared secrecy accelerates intimacy and friendship. This is the way it works on earth; this is also the way it works in our connection with heaven. Therefore, Jesus invites us to make it private.

When you make it private, you are setting yourself up for personal experiences with God. In the long lines of investment toward God, you will inevitably create private dialogue with him. Private dialogue leads to earned affection. Some people have a prayer room, others have a rocking chair on the front porch, but the key is a place where you can be alone with God. Private is where we learn the experience of his speaking voice.

When I first learned to dialogue with God, I took long walks. This habit has stayed with me for more than 40 years. Even when I pray indoors, I tend to pace. The essential is to be alone with God. This has the payoff of little distraction, the ability to talk out loud without the worry of being heard by others. It pulls my desire to know God out of the hazy cloud of good intentions and makes a bold statement to my soul and to God – "Oh God, you are my God; earnestly I seek you" (Psalm 63:1, ESV)

Susanna Wesley was the mother of John and Charles Wesley. In fact, she had nineteen children. Her years of raising a family were characterized by loss, hardship, and struggle. However, even in the busiest years of her life she kept the priority of prayer. The challenge for her was finding a place of privacy in a house filled with children. Her solution was to bring her Bible to her favorite chair and throw her long apron up over her head. This formed a make-shift tent. When the children saw the apron over her head, they knew she was meeting with God and was not to be disturbed. Through this unique practice of privacy, she preserved her priority of intimacy with God.

The limit of our private time with God is not defined by our circumstances, it is defined by our desire and personal resolve. We make time and space for the things we want the most.

Set aside Time: *But when you pray, go into your room, and shut the door*

Every strong relationship requires the honor of protected time. In our culture, this is one of the hardest things to do. We are resistant to block off time and give it to God, but when we protect our time with God, we are setting the table for his voice. This is nothing new. Every relationship will flourish when given protected time.

I met Mickey Edwards in kindergarten. We were fast friends even at that early age. We went through four years of high school together, a couple of years of college, and eventually married sisters. Even now, we usually talk at least once a week. As close as we are, I know that when I dedicate protected space to talk with him, it is then (and only then) that he is likely to tell me something that he would have otherwise kept to himself. It's not that he is prone to withhold; it is rather the simple fact that when I dedicate protected space to be with him, I am making myself available to hear his closest thoughts. Same with God. If I want to hear his closest thoughts, then I must pick a private place and protect the time.

I remember when the Atlanta Braves were dominating their conference from 1991 to 2005, winning 14 out of 15 conference titles. I was a fan and watched the Braves play most nights. For sure I would never miss a playoff game. However, one night I remember the unmistakable pull of God to come and meet with him. It just happened to be right as a playoff game was beginning. It may seem silly, but this was a test for me. I protested loudly in my soul, but I've learned God doesn't argue back. He invites me to turn aside to him and then the ball is in my court.

I exited my back door into the night air and my awareness of God's presence increased with every step. I don't think he is against baseball; I think he wanted to reign unchallenged in my affections. I chuckled as I walked past my neighbors' houses. I could hear the game announcers pouring out through open windows. I'll admit it was distracting trying to catch the score between the conversational spaces of my time with God. God had not required me to be undistracted. He asked me to turn aside, and I did. It was protected time dedicated to the Lord. The angst that I initially felt melted away as I stepped into his nearness. I couldn't tell you whether the Braves won that night, but I'll never forget making the decision to give God my treasured time. The fact that it felt costly made it that much sweeter.

Protected time and space are the proof of a prioritized relationship. This priority is the doorway to increased awareness of his presence. An increased awareness of his presence is the fountain from which his voice flows.

Cultivate relational familiarity: *But when you pray, go into your room, and shut the door and pray to your Father who is in secret.*

Every good relationship becomes familiar. When God characterized his relationship with us, he used the most familiar of relationships. He said that he is our Father in Heaven. In saying this, he reveals that we are supposed to be dependent upon him. We are to grow intimately familiar with him. We're not just to know about him or just to live a life for him, we are to know him personally; we're to encounter him repeatedly.

> "God is a Person . . . In making Himself known to us He stays by the familiar pattern of personality. He communicates with us through the avenues of our minds, our wills, and our emotions. The continuous and unembarrassed

interchange of love and thought between God and the soul of the redeemed man is the throbbing heart of the New Testament."[25]

The voice of God is relationally experienced. The way God interacts with us is in the stream of relational consciousness that we've been practicing with others our whole life. His voice is learned through familiarity. Not familiarity in the bored sense but familiar in the sense of someone loved whose presence is known through multiple experiences. The more experience, the more well-known— every nuance of their presence is an open book to the inward senses. You must learn to "pay attention to your attention for it is the doorway to encounter."[26]

I remember when I was in college and home for the summer. My brother who was four years older than me came in the basement door of our house at 2:00 a.m. It was pitch black. In a matter of an instant, I saw his silhouette recoil from the corner where I stood. He could not see me, but he could sense my presence there. He, of course, was startled, if not scared. He reached for the light and turned it on. Seeing me, he was relieved but slightly perturbed. The point is that though he could not see me, he was aware of my presence. What he experienced as fear, we experience as comfort and well-being as we grow to recognize the presence of God.

Spending time with God privately develops your ability to hear him in public: *But when you pray, go into your room, and shut the door and pray to your Father who is in secret. And your Father who sees in secret will reward you. (Matthew 6:6, ESV)*

Do you remember how obvious friend cliques were in the seventh grade? Without any formal declaration, everyone knew who was friends with whom because their friendship was public domain. In a similar fashion, as we become friends with God in private, others begin to take notice. Something is changing for the better, and it's only a matter of time before the reward of God's acquaintance surrounds your life. When that which is forged with God in private gains enough momentum, it will break into your public life. This is part of how God makes himself known to the world. Your private interaction with God has made you a carrier of his spiritual DNA. He is your reward.

The Truth: The Book for Listening

When our interaction with scripture dulls, so does our spiritual life. A life fueled by encounters with God is built upon an open Bible. I do not know anyone who has a catalog of stories with God who got there any other way. The Bible carries supernatural power to amplify the voice of God.

Logos and Rhema

Logos and Rhema are the New Testament Greek words translated as "Word." They point to two unique ways God speaks to us. Both *Logos* and *Rhema* mean "something said." But the nuance of *Logos* is that of a word already spoken and carrying an unchanging message, while the nuance of *Rhema* is the experience of a currently speaking voice. Something present tense.

These shades of color in the language help us see two ways God is speaking to us through the scriptures. He is unveiling a discourse about who He is, what He is like, His ways, His character, His story. It is objective and universal in its application. It is the same for everyone. This is *Logos*.

He speaks uniquely and directly to us as individuals. This is intimate and personal as an experience. This is *Rhema*.

This distinction helps me. When I read the scriptures, I am aware I'm learning objective facts about the story of God, His unchanging ways, His truth, and this IS GOD SPEAKING. But rarer and more precious are the moments when I'm aware that he is actively speaking to me in a moment of time. It's personal and meant only for me. It's one level of good to be given access to the story of God (open to all who will live an open-Bible life), but it's another level of good when the Lord of the scriptures pauses to look my way and speak directly to me.

This dynamic is not foreign to your life's experiences. Imagine you've taken a new position in a company. You show up for work and the first couple of days are spent in orientation. You are being schooled in the culture of the company. You may learn the history, you may learn procedures, you may learn expectations and benefits. This would be like Logos. Then there is a moment when your boss pulls you to the side and speaks directly to you. He or she gives you unique insight into your role, the potential they see in you, the hopes they have for your future. The personal conversation fits inside of the broader conversation about the company, but it is unique and profoundly meaningful because it was spoken only to you. This is like Rhema. These are the two conversations that are flowing out of scripture. God is continuously speaking through both.

Chronos and Kairos

The two Greek words found in the New Testament that are translated as "Time" are chronos and kairos. *Chronos* refers to chronological time. *Kairos* is the word for an opportune moment. Both are pointing toward our experience of time but each one indicates a different nuance from the other. Like *Logos* and *Rhema,* these two nuances are also indicators of the two ways God speaks.

Chronos

Like *Logos, Chronos* is pointing toward the objective unfolding of events in chronological time. In *Chronos time* we are learning the facts of the story of God. What happened and when. We learn the names of Adam and Eve's sons, we learn that Jesus healed on the Sabbath, we learn that God's throne is built on the foundation of righteousness and justice. Like *Logos, Chronos* is training us in objective fact. But do not be lulled to sleep. God is speaking. His story carries his voice.

Kairos

Kairos predictably aligns with the other conversation and the word Rhema. *Kairos* means *"an opportune moment."* It means a ripe point in time. It is that moment in time where something is possible because the time has finally come. Like Christmas morning, like election day, like your honeymoon night—a singular moment has arrived. Jesus stepped forward at the beginning of his public ministry and announced a *Kairos* moment when he said, "The time has come, the kingdom of God has come near!" *(*Mark 1:15, NIV*)* The word "time" in this declaration is *Kairos*. He is announcing the arrival of a long-anticipated day. The messiah is here! The Kingdom of Heaven has drawn near! Like a store announcing a long-awaited sale. Good deals abound right now! Like the red light at Krispy Kreme donuts, there is an opportunity for hot donuts right now. This opportunity will close at some point but for now it is an open invitation. This is *Kairos*.

Logos and *Chronos* are leading us to understand the facts, the story, the truth—God is speaking. *Rhema* and *Kairos* are leading us to personal encounters with God— an opportune moment has ripened, and God is speaking directly to me. We are a people of truth AND experience, a people of story AND encounter. We are being **trained by the objective conversation of scripture** (*Logos* and *Chronos*). We are being **tutored by the personal conversation with God** (*Rhema* and *Kairos*)

We were made for both conversations, and both are the voice of God in our lives. But the broader significance is that if we want to build a listening life, we must do so with an open Bible.

Seek God's voice with a daily opened Bible. Invest to know its stories. Invest to know its precepts. Don't be someone who quotes Ben Franklin and attributes it to the Bible. Don't be the one who mixes and matches narratives from the Bible. Be a learner of the scriptures. Invest time daily to know what's in the book. By doing this you are learning one aspect of the voice of God. But equally important, you are making yourself a candidate for the present tense voice of the Holy Spirit. The learner of the Logos receives the Rhema— meaning, the one who invests to know the scriptures hears God speak.

The Life: The Person Who is Speaking

"The Spirit-filled life is not a special, deluxe edition of Christianity. It is part and parcel of the total plan of God for his people."[27]

While I have put the role of the Holy Spirit buried deep into this chapter, the fact is, his importance in making God's Kingdom come alive is of the highest priority. The whole chapter, indeed, the whole book could be given to highlighting the Holy Spirit's essential place. The unfortunate truth is, many Christians make salvation through Jesus the end target rather than the starting line of their faith. "There are so many instances of arrested development in the church; believers who have settled into a condition of confirmed infancy, and whose testimony always begins back with conversion, and hovers around that event, like the talk of children who are perpetually telling how old they are. The scriptures seem to teach that there is a second stage in spiritual development, distinct and separate from conversion— sometimes widely separated in time from it and sometimes almost contemporaneous with it."[28]

This "second stage" is the charge of the Holy Spirit to the church.

The Holy Spirit is the person speaking. Without him, you will hear nothing. No atmospheres will change, no inward dialogue will form. We live under a sacred sky of heaven-sized possibilities but the daily choice to yield to his presence is ours. When we fail the yield test, we experience the prolonged silence of heaven. The blood of Jesus has purchased a million-acre inheritance, but you have chosen to live just on the border, bored with your one-acre experience.

God's Operating System
In the realm of computers, the operating system is the hub of all interaction. The computer is filled with incredible potential— applications and software capable of a speed and range of activity that previously (prior to the advent of computers) would have been impossible. But without an operating system there is no access to these useful powers. A computer without an operating system is dead and useless.

This absence of an operating system is like the experience of the pursuit of God without the presence of the Holy Spirit. If a connection that feels alive and important cannot be established, eventually we lose heart. Our vision for Kingdom living shrinks down to hopelessly human proportions. In that atmosphere of praying, God's voice seems like fiction— something we hear talked about in sermons but for our life there is no corresponding experience. How frustrating it would be to have a computer sitting on your desk, but you can't get it to spring to life. This is the way many see their Bible. But the Holy Spirit makes the connection between heaven and earth come to life. He turns our access to God into experience.

It's not complicated, but neither is it automatic. We are not built for the "one and done" moment of a sinner's prayer. We are designed for the life-long movement of an investor. A learner. An apprentice. A disciple. Remember that when John the Baptist was handing out clues to what God had in mind, he made two irresistible statements about Jesus:

1. **"Behold, the Lamb of God, who takes away the sin of the world!"** (John 1:29, ESV)

2. **"I (*John*) baptize you with water. But one who is more powerful than I will come, the straps of whose sandals I am not worthy to untie. He will baptize you with the Holy Spirit and fire."** (Luke 3:16, ESV)

These two declarations from scripture indicate the twofold life that Christ has accomplished for me and you. Statement one is Christ's work for me: my sins removed. My identity changed. My citizenship transferred. Heaven is my home.

Statement two is Christ's work in me: my life baptized by the Holy Spirit. Head to toe "wet" but not with water, but with the fire of heaven's passions. Possibility unrestricted. To have this kind of life the Holy Spirit must be received, expected, and fully acted upon.

The obedient sacrifice of Jesus on the cross and his subsequent resurrection is a redeeming work that is complete. You and I cannot add to it. Eternity will put Jesus at the center of the story. He is the King and there is no other. However, the last instructions that Jesus left with his disciples let them know there is more. Yes, your sin debt has been eradicated. You are justified before God as if you never sinned. You've been purchased at a great price and have been grafted into the inheritance of God. But this same Jesus, before he went to the cross, set up a future expectation for more.

The disciples must have been slightly confused. How could it be better for us if Jesus leaves? But that's what Jesus said,

"I tell you the truth: it is to your advantage that I go away, for if I do not go away, the Helper will not come to you. But If I go, I will send him." (John 16:7, ESV)

The last thing He told the disciples was: "Do not leave Jerusalem, but wait for the gift my Father promised, which you have heard me speak about. For John baptized with water, but in a few days, you will be baptized with the Holy Spirit." (Acts 1:4-5, NIV)

The promise of the Holy Spirit was a promise for One to be sent that would be exactly like Jesus, but now, not only *with* the disciples but dwelling *inside* of them. With this shift, the invitation of God extends by leaps and bounds.

When God delivered the Israelites from their slavery in Egypt, a pillar of fire by night and a pillar of cloud by day housed the presence of God. From this cloud of fire, Israel was led by God himself.[29] With the promise of the Holy Spirit, the fire that the Israelites could only enjoy as exterior to themselves was now promised to dwell on the inside. For those who covenant with God through Jesus, the dwelling of the Holy Spirit is the completion of our spiritual operating system.

It is a shortcoming in the church when we invite the world to the cross but make little or no invitation to Pentecost. The empty grave has purchased a promise of an indwelling Holy Spirit that is present tense, but it is not automatic. It is a completion that progresses forward through the continued dynamic of asking and receiving. It is an observable fact that many "receive" Jesus but fail to know, pursue, or receive the active role of the Holy Spirit. Such is the story of Boston's AJ Gordon (1836 – 1895), who was a pastor, preacher, writer, composer and founder of Gordon College and Gordon-Conwell Theological Seminary. He writes of his own journey of awakening to the Holy Spirit's presence, not from the position of a lost sinner but as a redeemed son. Furthermore, already engaged in full-time ministry as a pastor, he writes of his journey of powerless discouragement:

> "Well do we remember those days when drudgery was pushed to the point of desperation. The hearers must be moved to repentance and confession of Christ; therefore, more effort must be devoted to the sermon . . . then came the disappointment that few, if any, were converted by all this which had cost a week of solid toil. And now attention was turned to the prayer meeting as the possible seat of the difficulty— so few attending it and so little readiness to participate in its services. Alas, there is no increase in the attendance, and instead of spontaneity in prayer and witnessing there is silence which seems almost

like sullenness! . . . Thus, the burdens of anxiety increase while we are trying to lighten them, and should-be helpers become hinderers, till discouragement comes and sleepless nights ensue."

"It was after all of this" he continued "of which even the most intimate of friends knew nothing, that there came one day a still voice of admonition, saying, **"There standeth one among you whom ye know not"**. And perhaps I answered, "Who is he, Lord, that I might know him?" I had known the Holy Ghost as a heavenly influence to be invoked, but somehow, I had not grasped the truth that he is a Person of the Godhead who came down to earth at a definite time and who has been in the church ever since, just as real as Jesus was here during the thirty and three years of his earthly life.[30]

Empowered by receiving and expecting

The Holy Spirit empowers us for a life of Kingdom involvement. He transforms us inwardly through daily surrender, and he qualifies us for impossible outward accomplishments. He gives gifts and invites us to follow the supernatural example of Jesus.

It is on this point we often fall short. The Holy Spirit gets relegated to his token position in our creed, but no active acceptance is put in play.

We "believe" in his power, but we have little spiritual power ourselves. We idolize the heroes of the bible, but we do not expect the radical exploits of their lives to manifest through us. We tried once or twice to pray for something impossible but turned back due to failure. Our expectation got wobbly knees due to a weakly formed resolve. Discouragement came for a visit, and we began to shift our theology rather than strengthen our resolve, lowering our expectations to stave off intimidation.

But the outcome is costly. The church is weak and unimpressive. Our lives are lonely and broken. The world looks to the church for God-sized outcomes but instead often finds a gathering of fleshly weaklings with contrived theology.

Yet, in bold contrast to this, Jesus gave the simple admonition:
"If you then, though you are evil, know how to give good gifts to your children, how much more will your Father in heaven give the Holy Spirit to those who ask him!" (Luke 11:13, ESV)

Those who want a life led by the voice of God must ask, receive, and believe upon the promise that Jesus made. Reckon upon the Holy Spirit's presence.

AJ Gordon resolved:

> "On the whole, and after prolonged study of the Scripture we cannot resist this conviction: As Christ, the second person of the Godhead, came to earth to make atonement for sin and to give eternal life, and as sinners must receive

him by faith in order to have forgiveness and sonship, so the Holy Spirit, the third person of the Godhead, came to earth to communicate the 'power from on high;' and we must as believers in like manner receive him by faith in order to be qualified for service. Both gifts have been bestowed, but it is not what we have but what we know that we have by a conscious appropriating faith, which determines our spiritual wealth."[31]

Let's pause here to make sure the weight of that statement sinks in. Let me re-write it in my own words: **It's not our access to the Holy Spirit that is in question. It's our personal experience of the Holy Spirit. It's the demonstration of our personal receiving and expanding expectation upon the Holy Spirit that proves our spiritual power.**

The whole ecosystem of God operates at our will – it must be received. A gift opened. A fire daily tended. An ever-expanding Kingdom— not done to us but released through us. At the center of the fire— the voice of God.

Wrapping it up

From the simplest action of just showing up for prayer to the most mystic regions of our beliefs about the Holy Spirit, everything must be tended, watched over and lived. There are no spare parts in the Kingdom. Every invitation from heaven is meant to amplify the voice of God. Any door of invitation left unopened or unattended turns down the volume. Or more accurately reduces our ability to hear. Each invitation from God is a Kingdom current that works hand in glove with the others to bring me into the presence of a God delighted to have me speak with him and willing to speak back.

Invocation

Next Step:
Ask the Holy Spirit to speak to you

Scripture:
"But the Advocate, the Holy Spirit, whom the Father will send in my name, will teach you all things and will remind you of everything I have said to you." (John 14)

Let me hear what God the Lord will speak, for he will speak peace to his people (Psalm 85:8)

Quote:
Lucy woke out of the deepest sleep you can imagine, with the feeling that the voice she liked best in the world had been calling her name. (C.S. Lewis, <u>the Chronicles of Narnia</u>)

The realm of his presence becomes our greatest inheritance, and divine encounters our greatest memories. (Bill Johnson, <u>Dreaming with God</u>)

Prayer:
Father, I want to know you. Not just know about you; I want to experience you. I want to hear your voice. You alone hold the words that I need to hear. I pause before you and spread my life out at your feet. As I seek you in private, lead me by the sound of your voice in my chest. Thank you for the scriptures. Bring them to life as I read. Holy Spirit, I receive your presence. Immerse me into the Kingdom of Jesus! Adorn my life with your character and fill my efforts with your power.

Chapter 5
Keep Rhythm

Cover all the necessary conversations

Mary Anne and I are working on thirty-six years together now. She is all wonderful and more than I deserve. A few days ago, however, I sensed that she was discontent. There were words brewing just beneath the surface and it was only a matter of time before they would need to be said. The space between us was growing cloudy. I may not know the reason for her discontentment but soon we'd need to talk. Like everybody else, we married to be together— to enjoy the passing of days and the engagement of life with a vibrant pulse. Something shared —alive, smiling, laughing. But life conspires against these noble goals. This cloud visits everyone's house. To get through to the other side requires staying present, being honest, sharing boldly and having all the necessary conversations.

Prayer carries these same challenges and requires the same resolve. I realize that it doesn't make sense to picture God as discontent. He is fully self-sufficient and needs nothing. However, he has made himself vulnerable to me, for this is how love works. Every important relationship has seasons of change, moments of challenge, both heights and depths. Prayer is how I keep my focus on the current status of my relationship with him. All of the breakdowns in the relationship come from my side (more on that in the next chapter), but the relational stream between us is alive. It is not a one-size-fits-all dynamic.

The path of prayer— like the marriage relationship – is perseverant, intimate, and committed for the long haul to the mutual benefit of the union. It is not for those with a weak resolve, it is not for the distracted, and it most certainly is not for the silent. Silence is the ground where estrangement grows. It leaves the gate open for usurpers like contempt, suspicion, offense, distance. Words need to be said, but not just any words—the right words for the right moment. Prayer needs fearless words inside of important conversations. Not random and rare but part of a healthy rhythm that covers multiple genres of life.

As you already know, relationships require different kinds of conversations. One kind of conversation for a dinner date, a different kind of conversation for a budget discussion. One kind for the bedroom, a different one for the ballgame. Just like normal life, we must choose to keep a rhythm of prayer that makes sense. A rhythm that covers every important sector of life. Prayers that flow at different speeds at different times. The conversation depends on the moment I'm standing in. There must be different kinds of prayer covering all the possible moods of life, spanning all the changing situations. Desires and disappointments all come into play. The wider the field of conversation with Heaven, the broader the relational experience with God on Earth.

Keeping Rhythm

We all know what it's like to fall out of rhythm in a relationship. The person who had a dedicated place in the orbit of our life has drifted to the outer rim. When this happens, most of our time is spent just catching up. Catching up carries the tone of just getting current. In a perpetual mode of catch up, it's hard to prosper and move forward. It's the same with God in prayer. Prayer flourishes when it's consistent. Maintaining rhythm produces that consistency; consistency, then, keeps the relationship current. But what are the different rhythms of prayer? What are the areas of our earthly existence that should be attended to in prayer? What keeps me current with God?

"Love the Lord your God with all your heart, with all your soul, and with all your mind, and with all your strength." (Mark 12:30, ESV)

Worship Rhythm
Love the Lord with all your heart

In western church culture, worship has come to be synonymous with singing. The truth is, though, singing is just one form of worship. Worship takes many forms but what is its essential DNA? Worship is honoring God for who He is. It is celebrating Him for what He has done and what He is yet to do. It is giving God my personal "yes" in surrender and response to all the above. So, the acts of worship may take many forms but what never changes is who God is and what He has done. And above all, no authentic worship takes place in me until I give my yes to God. This resetting of my yes to God is a reoccurring rhythm. Worship is a verb. It is a relational reflex that is built overtime with high intentionality. Worship prayer is the rhythm of prayer I use to open my heart to God.

The cornerstone of deep friendship is the heart— the co-mingling of one spirit with another. Even when our earthly relationships evolve from acquaintance to friend, the difference-maker is that shared center of our being. Those who are most dear are given the most access. But hearts do not stay in the open position by default. In fact, mine tends to close off and become solitary without much effort at all. An open heart is a choice. Worship is the necessary rhythm I use to push open the gates of my locked-down center.

Priority

Unlike all our other relationships, by his nature, God is first. He created our hearts for himself. There is a throne inside each of us where only God is suited to reign. He is irrevocably first. But to us he has given the right to choose him second. When we put him second, he doesn't suffer any loss. Not so for us. We are personally unhinged by the maneuver. In due time, our lives begin to dismantle. "Put God First" is more than a bumper sticker, it's more than a lesson for Sunday school, it is perhaps the most reliable coaching advice that could ever be given to keep one's life in order.

At first glance this may seem superficial. On paper perhaps it looks obligatory. But if I engage authentically in giving God first place in my heart, the experience is transforming. It leads me into outcomes that I can't find any other way. It awakens my heart and brings my inner world into order. But the rule is firm: the priority of first place belongs to God. The rhythm of worship praying is dedicated to making sure that he has first place in me.

Affection

When affection is taken for granted, it is the beginning of a downhill slide. True in life, true in prayer. Worship rhythms safeguard against this inevitable tendency.

Later today I'm leaving on a trip to the north Georgia mountains. I'm taking a two-day getaway trip with Mary Anne. Nobody else is invited. It is time set aside to reconnect the affection that we carry towards each other. She will endure staying in a rustic setting, I will likely endure walking through little gift shops in small mountain towns. But it's just us. We will write another page in the book of love. Our affection will be refreshed and made current. Worship prayers similarly set aside time with God just to give him affection.

My friend, pastor Kevin Myers, calls this kind of prayer "lost time with God." Like many of you, he keeps a busy schedule and realizes the tendency to "fit God in" must be arrested. He replaces that tendency with the rhythm of intentionally slowing his life down. Blocking off some time to have no agenda other than to connect affectionately with God. He puts it this way,

> "The best conversations happen when we are not watching the clock. Whether marriage, family, or friendship – all relationships tend this way. They flourish when given room to breathe, they flow more freely when they are not constrained by time. Lost time means setting aside a portion of time big enough and well positioned in the rhythms of my life so that I am not pulled by the gravity of the next thing on my list. It is a place where re-connecting my heart to God is the only thing on my list."

For him this means scheduling whole days, a month in advance, for lost time with God. Maybe your life (with some aggressive calendar adjustments) will allow you to do the same. But if not, maybe you can protect an hour or so every few days. The portion of time will be consistent with the allowances of your life. But be careful that you do not use your "busy schedule" as an excuse to live small with God. Accept the plain truth right now— everyone is busy. Everyone has "unmovable" obstacles in their life. The fact is, we all make room for the things that are most important to us. The placement of God in your schedule will be set by the level of desire that you carry for Him.

> "If we are honest, we already do lost time in a lot of ways in our life. None of us have extra-time but we find time to binge watch Netflix, or we find four hours to give to a

round of golf. There is nothing wrong with any of these things. But we must come face to face with the truth that God has promised to be found by us, but he will not be found cheaply, sitting on the back burner of our priorities. If I can't find lost time to give to him then I can't expect to get lost in him."[32]

When our heart connects intimately with God it sets the tone for all our other interactions with Him. Jesus modeled this often praying through the night. We don't need to aspire to his quantity of prayer. We aspire to his quality of relationship with God as Father. As the relationship grows, our rhythm of lost time with God will deepen.

Walking Rhythm
"With all your soul"

When Mary Anne and I had been married less than two months we found out that she was pregnant with our first baby. We were both happy but stunned by this development. The timing was sudden and unexpected. Like any young married couple, we were still working our way through the complexities of our first year of marriage. Trying to figure out our calling, our careers, and just adjust to living together, the pregnancy brought 24-7 sickness for Mary Anne. It brought pressure to my work status. It was a bewildering season. My soul was full of questions, doubts, fears, and a robust feeling of inadequacy. As it turns out, this is a ripe atmosphere for speaking with God.

I would arrive at our rented duplex bone-tired from a long day of commissioned sales. Mary Anne would do her best to put a good face on her nausea and we'd try to enjoy each other's company. After a couple of hours my desperation would catch up with me and I would walk out into the night air to make my petitions heard on high. There was nothing religiously correct about my approach to God. I just walked and talked. I let the flow of uncertainties find voice and I spoke with God. I didn't worry about getting it right, I just had to get it out. I found that he would meet me in the honesty. I can't say that I got tons of answers to my 26-year-old questions, but I found the comfort of God with me. I wasn't alone. That was enough to help me survive the uncertainty of that season.

This is a picture of the walking rhythm of prayer. It is the rhythm of prayer where I survey the landscape of my soul. I unpack the traffic in my mind, confront the stubbornness of my will, and corral the full range of emotions roaming the hills of my soul. It is the rhythm for drawing out into the open before God the mental usurpers sitting in the background noise of my thoughts. It is for choosing to soften my will toward God. It is for coming to terms with how I really feel and bringing it to God. It is the rhythm for assessing my mental well-being and bringing every rogue thought back into submission to Christ.

This rhythm of prayer is an ongoing journey; I never fully arrive. This rhythm is constantly needed to keep my life headed in the right direction with God— thus the name *Walking prayer*. I am daily walking out the contents of my soul before God in prayer. Perhaps the easiest way to understand the role of our soul is by the personal pronoun *me*. It is the very busy hub of my consciousness, typically thought of as mind, will, and emotion. Jesus knew that we'd have a daily need for this hub to be surrendered, ordered and cleaned up. These three acts are the solution side of the problem. In other words, there are many ways that my will, my thoughts, and emotions go astray, but the spiritual resolution always comes back to a combination of surrender, order and cleaning my spiritual house.

Prayer is less like a trip to the doctor's office and more like an exercise program. Not a place I go to "fix me" but a way I do life to stay well and to stay connected. It's not the view at the top of the mountain so much as it is the walk itself.

"Therefore, as you received Christ Jesus the Lord, so walk in him." (Colossians 2:6, ESV)
"Look carefully then how you walk, not as unwise but as wise" (Ephesians 5:15, ESV)
"Walk in a manner worthy of the Lord, fully pleasing to him" (Colossians 1:10, ESV)

Surrender
Spiritual closeness with God is always an altar of surrender. Some may prefer the word submission. Either way, laying down my will and picking up God's way is the front door to intimacy with Him. I may, on occasion, wish this was a one and done exercise, but it's not. Closeness with God

calls for daily vigilance. Walking Prayer understands that my mind, will, and emotions have an arc of their own, a path managed by self-interest. It's about who is in charge.

Jesus prescribes a daily surrender:

"If anyone would come after me, let him deny himself and take up his cross daily and follow me." (Luke 9:23, NIV)

Sometimes, taking up the cross can go quickly, sometimes it takes longer to untangle my soul and talk out its issues. Clearly, if I stay current with God, things tend to go quicker. It's like a horse farmer once told me as we walked toward his barn.

"You ever heard of the feed bucket principle?"

"No sir."

"Well, a feed bucket is like our soul. When I feed these horses there is a residue of grain that gets stuck on the side of the bucket. If I wash out the bucket every day after feeding, that residue comes right out. But if I fail to clean out the bucket and it accumulates for several days in a row it hardens. The only way to get it clean once it hardens is with a wire brush."

He paused and looked at me for effect.

"You ever had the Lord take a steel brush to you?"

I got his point. My soul needs daily tending. If I neglect this, my soul pollutes and clogs with the residue of living life. That which may go away quickly when tended daily can turn into wire brush sessions when neglected. Nobody wants that.

Jesus promised that we could have living water flowing up from internal wells, but I've got to lower the bucket of my soul down into the water of his presence, the water of his word, and allow both to shape my mind, will, and emotions.

Order

When God gets first place, my soul begins to come into order. I do not mean the perfect resolve of all of my outward circumstances, but the inward alignment of my thoughts, feelings, and convictions. The disarray of scattered thoughts, untethered emotion, and willful selfishness begins to dissolve in favor of better companions. A sense of being valued by heaven calms the striving. The awareness of God's love welcomes me in. Well-being accompanies closeness with God. As I bend my soul toward Him, I am restored to order that is experienced as peace. My mind, will, and emotion bow to the higher vision of a life submitted to God. In a strange twist of God's economy, I am most free when I surrender.

I live on a small horse farm in north Georgia. My experience with horses reminds me of my inner world with God. Horses are naturally very resistant to being caught and bridled. And while they look beautiful when they are roaming free, there is a level of beauty that takes over when they yield to their master. My horse, Astro, is short, pure white, and full of energy. He is beautiful standing in the pasture, wind blowing through his mane. But when he gets bridled and under saddle, he is glorious. He is impressive, and he knows it. The submission that he resists is actually the path that leads him to find a greater purpose. This reminds me of my life with God. The way I resist coming to God in prayer reminds me of those days when Astro gets stubborn. Like Astro, my greatest glory and my sense of purpose increase as I yield to the Master. The rhythm of Walking Prayer is my self-imposed "bridle" and "saddle."

My soul is like a house whose furniture is sat in and moved around each day. Many things contribute to the disarray. Through prayer I put the furniture back into the arrangement preferred by the Lord Jesus, the Master of the House. Then there is peace because order has been restored.

Working Rhythm
"With all your mind and all your strength."

When the Lord God created mankind, he put us in a garden and ordained work. We've been working ever since. Not just the work we get paid to do, but hundreds of other endeavors that make life meaningful. We write stories, join clubs, repair our houses, climb mountains, volunteer at the PTA, learn an instrument, cultivate friendship, and a hundred other kinds of "work" that make us human. We make things, grow things, accomplish results. God invested the work instinct in us and we spend most of our time pursuing things that produce results.

Working prayer is the rhythm of prayer where I review the things I'm invested in. The work of my life needs wisdom to solve problems. It involves making decisions about direction. I sift through my desires, and I aim my life at accomplishment. Nothing too small to bring to his attention. Nothing too big to dream about.

He is the Master, and I am a steward of his Kingdom. I am responsible for how I handle this commission. In the working rhythm of prayer, I imagine God as my employer, and I am the regional manager, entrusted with the work of his company in the place where I live. I come before God with the mentality of an employee entrusted with the success of the kingdom in my region. My time of prayer is my chance to bring before the owner of the company all the agendas that need attention for the success of the company in my region. I am respectful but bold, focused, and honest as I process with him the challenges confronting me. I ask for things, specific things. And sometimes I make a case for why I think it's important. None of us would show up for a meeting unprepared with the owner of the company. How much more the Owner of all kingdoms? Yes, He is my Father, but He nevertheless expects a return on his investment in me. How do I build a working rhythm in prayer?

Direction

One of the potholes of prayer is our tendency to relegate prayer to the religious corner of our life and fail to bring the "nuts and bolts" of our life to God. We easily get stuck praying for some general sense of God's will but fail to sift the actual specifics of what we are working on in our life. The whole point of "working prayer" is that prayer can change outcomes and help set a new and preferred direction.

Not happy with your career? Pray. Not happy in your marriage relationship? Talk to God about it. Not happy with how things are going with your children? Let Heaven hear your parental complaint! A car repair got you distracted? Mention it to God. Got an idea for a business?

Ask God about it. You get the point. I shape my prayers around the direction of my work.

Focus

The ability to turn what occupies my mind into prayer is harder than you think. It's easy to obsess, but hard to structure those obsessive thoughts into prayers. Harder still is the ability to construct them into important, repeatable prayers. Important and repeatable prayers are powerful because they give me "hand-holds" to remember previous conversations with God. Perhaps I settled a conviction —write it down. Perhaps I said a feeling in a perfect sentence— write it down. Writing it down gives me a way to funnel back to a previous conversation that needs more attention. And in the long lines of seeing something done through prayer, one of the tools I've often used is called a "prayer well."

Prayer wells are simple outlines of prayer that cover the major sectors of my life's activity. For instance: prayers about my calling, prayers concerning my family, my personal development, etc. The outline sections do not matter as much as the fact that I'm using the outline to funnel my prayers in important directions.

I realize that this sounds a little mechanical, but I've found that an important prayer captured and written down is like gold. It has the power to quickly escort me to the place of stirred desire with God. Prayer wells keep me from wasting time trying to figure out what I want to talk to God about. Prayer wells keep focus streamlined enough to create spiritual momentum. Over a period of six months, I can have the assurance that I've stayed consistent in asking God for the same outcomes in prayer.

The prayer wells are not the focus— they are a tool to help maintain focus. For me, loving the Lord with all my mind and strength is greatly assisted with some organization.

This outlined approach to praying may seem too mechanical to be personal. I have found the opposite to be true. The prayer well keeps my focus trained on the things that matter most. Furthermore, the determiner of whether prayer is personal and intimate versus mechanical, and rote is not the mode of prayer that I'm using. It's my internal posture. If I'm feeling mechanical, the problem is not the prayer agenda, it's me.

However, if prayer gets so absorbed in the mechanical that I've lost intimacy then I intentionally add some mystery through worship prayer (or whatever adds heart for you). If prayer feels like it's stalled because you got lost in the mystery, then add the mechanical intention of outlined Working Prayers. It's a little bit science and a little bit art, a little bit math and a little bit music. It can be organized but it must be organic. It is predictable yet remains unscripted.

Petition
"God has made himself vulnerable to the desires of his people"[33]

Petition is a word usually reserved for legal requests or a list of names gathered in support of some initiative. But I am using the word in its scriptural context, such as,
"Do not be anxious about anything, but in every situation, by prayer and petition, with thanksgiving, present your requests to God." (Philippians 4:6, NIV)

Petition means to ask with a potent desire for an outcome. It means desire not dulled with pseudo-humility but surprisingly sharp enough to be felt in Heaven. If you think of a small child who has fastened onto the desire to have a friend come over for the afternoon, or for some simple indulgence from the ice cream shop, then you are getting closer to the single-minded focus that petition requires. A child in this frame of desire is likely to fall to pieces if their request is denied. They will be heard. Their desire will be known. They will not go quietly.

The writer of Hebrews positions Jesus in this posture of prayer when he says, "he offered up prayers and petitions with fervent cries and tears" (Hebrews 5:7, NIV). I don't picture Jesus as a spoiled child and neither should you, but we should wake up and notice that he carried desire in prayer sufficient for fervent cries and weeping.

"What do you want?"

This is not a question that God avoids. In fact, he includes it in the prayer ecosystem on purpose. He leans toward your answer. Do not doubt that this is true. You need look no further than the conversations Jesus had with those in need. He may have known what they needed, but he required them to say it. He walked right to the center of their need and asked, "What do you want me to do for you?" (Matthew 3:32, NIV)

We shouldn't be surprised by this. Isn't this the way most of us parent? Aren't we susceptible to the desires of our children? But we want them to own up to their desires. The size of this thought when applied to our prayer movement is so gigantic that once we consider it, we either back down, too intimidated by the size of it, or our vision of prayer changes forever.

Your desire is a pivotal fulcrum in God's Kingdom economy. You will not likely get everything you desire, but you are nevertheless invited to ask in prayer. It is through this candor of desire that you are inwardly shaped.

Pretense is the opposite. Pretense tempts us to shape prayer by what we think it should sound like. It is the very core of dead religion and causes everything to go stale. But true desire honestly shared gives God the raw material for our transformation into His image. God is not trying to control us into moral conformity; he is reframing our inner world. As he does, our desires begin to take shape around his influence. As our desires progressively shape around God's presence, he invites us to engage those desires back to him through petitioning prayer. In doing so, prayer becomes a stewardship where my desires turn into kingdom outcomes.

God intends to fill the earth with the experience of his presence. This will be accomplished not by religious pretense, but through the path of authentic interaction with God by the church. Day upon day, week after week, months added up into holy years. Our desires maturing into sacred life purpose until the kingdoms of this world become the Kingdoms of our Lord and of His Christ.

Keeping Rhythm through Conversational Doorways: The Lord's Prayer

When the disciples asked Jesus how they should pray, he gave them the Lord's prayer. Wasn't that the perfect script for praying? Indeed, Jesus gave us the Lord's prayer but not as a script. It is a prayer given to us to outline the recurring conversations of prayer. Each line is like a relational doorway that is a conversation starter. The Lord's Prayer is a framework for keeping rhythm in a way that aims our apprentice journey with Jesus appropriately. As we follow its flow to create conversation with God, we naturally find ourselves talking about the right things.

For example:

"Our Father who is in Heaven"

This is not for daily recitation. It is a doorway of conversation to remind me that I am on earth, and he is in heaven. He holds all the power; I do not. The "Our Father" line of the Lord's prayer is an invitation to remember again who God is and who he invites me to be with him. "Father" reminds me that God positions Himself as my keeper, but not from a distance— like a good father, close and presiding over my life. While this phrase of the prayer is only six words, it is a doorway of conversation that could last much longer.

Every line of the Lord's prayer may be seen the same way – a doorway that opens a topic of conversation. It is a prayer outline itself.

"Your Kingdom come; your will be done on earth as it is in Heaven"

Like we discussed in the rhythm of Walking Prayer, this doorway of conversation is where I freshly surrender my path to his will. And also, like the rhythm of Working Prayer, where I co-labor with God to call down his purposes into the realities of earth. It's not a script; it's a portal of dialogue that expands the relationship.

"Give us this day our daily bread" is the doorway for processing our needs. No need is too small, no dream is too big. Though this is a short part of the overall prayer, I am invited to spend as much time here as I want. Usually, this doorway of prayer rests in the stream of Walking Prayer. Dropping off my worries about provision and making my requests known.

"Forgive us our trespasses as we forgive those who trespass against us" is the conversation of humbling myself and admitting my sins before God. Not a recitation— a conversation. Not a court of accusation, but an honest assessment of my character and conduct with a rescuing God who is ready to forgive a sinner like me.

"Lead us not into temptation but deliver us from evil" This doorway of conversation reminds me that while God has invited me to live inside a love story, the setting of that story is war. I have a spiritual adversary who is seeking to kill me, steal from me, and destroy the things that I love. The scripture says that he is my accuser, not just once in a while but day and night. This prayer conversation is where I come into God's court and petition for protection from his diabolical attempts to ruin me.

"For yours is the kingdom and the power and the glory forever" is the conversational doorway for remembering that this story is not about me. God is preeminent and my life is kept safe as he is kept in its center. Most of the time I begin in worship and that is how I conclude. But it wasn't my idea, it's right here in the Lord's Prayer – God's outline for praying.

If you are struggling to recapture your rhythm with God, use the Lord's Prayer and give yourself permission to spend as long as you need to at any of the conversational doorways contained in it.

God is not manageable, but your relationship with him must be tended. The wise follower of Jesus will design a multi-faceted approach to prayer. By doing so, strong threads of experience will anchor your relationship and keep you moving forward with God.

Invocation

Next Step:
Build a rhythm for your relationship with God. Have all the necessary conversations.
Scripture:
And when you pray, do not use vain repetitions as the heathens do. (Matthew 6:7)

Quote:
You don't have to swing hard to hit a home run. If you got the timing, it'll go. (Yogi Berra)

Prayer:
Father, keep me from getting lost inside of religious activity. Help me to steer clear of a life that looks good on the outside but on the inside is a vacant lot. Help me to keep a rhythm that honors my relationship with you. I know that you can handle my doubt, my anger, my fear, confusion, and questions. Steer me toward the conversation that we need to have today. Renew me under the waterfall of your presence and help me lay out my life before you one honest conversation at a time.

Section Three: See it Through
MATURE TOWARD SHARED PURPOSES WITH GOD

We live in temporary times. We change our minds almost as often as we change our clothes. Patient industry has bowed to anxious haste. Earth has become a place where we leave behind instead of seeing it through. Our ability to commit and finish has wobbly legs. To see it through to the end, prayer must mature..

Chapter 6
HIKE THE DISTANCE

When prayer becomes broken

Recently I sat on my front porch with a friend whom I'd watched grow up in our church, but I hadn't seen in several years. I asked him how his relationship with God was faring. With meek resignation he admitted, "I gave that up a long time ago." We processed for a few minutes. There was sadness in his story. Family struggles, faith slowly deconstructing, shifting community. Under the weight of these disappointments, he had drifted into a different view of life. But he was not better off for those choices. His life wasn't richer from the shift. He was decidedly less hopeful and just getting by. I did not lack compassion for how things had gone, but I couldn't help but wonder how much better life would be for him if he would see his relationship with God through to the other side.

Relationships break down. At some point, prayer will too.

Over time and through different seasons, distance creeps in.

In human relationships it looks like this, whether a spouse or a friend, it's that moment when you can feel the distance. Where there was once focused attention and a natural ease of interaction, now the conversation feels forced. You get the feeling that the relationship is just going through the motions. The heart is left cold in the presence of the one who has always been a source of warmth. These seasons are not fun. They lead us to feel taken for granted by the other, or sometimes, leave us feeling like the relationship has changed and we are not as interested as we used to be. The vital question is this: Will you give yourself permission to indulge the breakdown or will you honestly confront it?

This same question applies to our relationship with God in prayer. Distance will occur and we will either allow it or confront it. You may protest and say, "When earthly relationships break down, I confront the other person, I can't do that with God." First, yes you can. But before we step into confronting God, let's admit that the first step in repairing distance is a step in the direction of ourselves. Our first instinct is to blame the other person. But we need to always examine ourselves first. This is a powerful rule of relationship and Jesus served it to us clearly, "Why do you look at the speck of sawdust in your brother's eye and pay no attention to the plank in your own eye?" (Matthew 7:3)

I grew up playing baseball. Though I never played in the outfield, I know the first rule of catching a fly ball. Your first step is always backwards. Your eyes and every instinct prompt you to step forward but if you heed your feelings, you are very likely to have the ball fly over your head. In baseball terms, you turned what should have been a routine out into an extra base hit for the other team. When breakdowns come, if we want to deal with the distance, we must take a step backwards and start with ourselves. I must admit that my first instinct is to blame God, or circumstances, or any number of other scapegoats. But taking a step back means that I resist my natural instinct and admit that I am where prayer breaks down. This is not condemnation; it is the realization that my life resists coming to God. Inward usurpers erode the foundation of my love for God. Learning to get past these prayer breakdowns means learning how to confront the sources of my own resistance.

Distraction

I'm busy. I've got a lot going on. My schedule is packed, and yet I still carry a low-grade fear of missing out. If I'm honest, there is mild anxiety that is attached to my full schedule, but instead of coming to God to address the anxiousness, I create diversions.

Distraction is a major component of prayer breakdown. I check Instagram one more time. I take another stroll through Facebook or YouTube. I pull into another episode of Netflix, I step into the oblivion of gaming, I send one more work-related email. No guilt intended, just the reality that many things battle for my attention. If I do not self-manage my distractions, then distance will appear in my relationship with God. To see my relationship with God through to the end, I will have to confront distraction.

Disappointment

We are a race of the disappointed. Maybe you prayed at a key moment in your past, and it did not turn out the way you thought it should? Maybe there was a church that let you down? Maybe it was an important leader in your life who proved to be deeply flawed? These (and a thousand other reasons) cause us to put God at a distance because we are disappointed. Our trust was broken, God didn't seem to hold up his end of the deal, and so we close off our heart. It's hard to be offended at someone and maintain an open heart.

We all have seasons in our life when we are tempted to say, "If God was coming for me, he'd already be here by now," or "If God loves me then this would have never happened." These statements rise from the soul that is suffering. The Psalms are full of bitter disappointment, but they also point the way through the sadness. Go to God with the letdown; don't shut him out.

Life on Earth will be disappointing. It comes with the territory. Jesus warned us:

"In this world you will have trouble but take heart. I have overcome the world." (John 16:33, NIV) In saying this, He is redirecting our disappointments back toward heaven^ to again remember God's disposition toward us.

I must choose to trust God in disappointing uncertainty. All relationships lean this way. There are seasons where misunderstanding abounds, and trust is required. Disappointment will come. When it does, I can pray: "You've got all the power and I'm disappointed with how you are treating me." A better prayer by far would be, "You've got all the power. In your kindness would you help me, deliver me, heal me?"

I love the declaration of Shadrach, Meshach, and Abednego from the book of Daniel. They had suffered great disappointment. They were conquered exiles. Disappointment would be an understatement. Disappointment turned to threat as the King demanded that they bow to worship him or else. To the King's dire threat, they responded with clarity,

> "We do not need to defend ourselves before you in this matter. If we are thrown into the blazing furnace, the God we serve is able to deliver us from it, and he will deliver us from Your Majesty's hand. But even if he does not, we want you to know, Your Majesty, that we will not serve your gods or worship the image of gold you have set up."
> (Daniel 3:16-18, NIV)

They could have folded to fear and bowed to the image of the king. They could have become offended at God saying, "Are you kidding me! We have continued to serve you faithfully. We've tried to do the right things and our lives seem to go from bad to worse." Like the offended sandlot kid who took his bat and ball and went home. He broke up the game because things didn't go his way. But Shadrach, Meshach, and Abednego understood that in our disappointments God's goodness is not on trial, our maturity is.

Shadrach, Meshach, and Abednego did get thrown into the blazing furnace. And the story could have ended there. But it did not. They were thrown into the fire, and God appeared in the fire to stand next to them. They emerged from the furnace whole. Not only were they brought through safely, but God's reputation was powerfully displayed through their story.

We may encounter deep disappointment, but when we do, we have the invitation to stay engaged with God in prayer. The invitation is to live in the expectation that we will emerge whole from the furnace – to walk through fire but not be consumed.

To hike the distance with God I will have to come to grips with disappointment and take the risk of continued trust.

Disbelief
Faith is the spark that accelerates prayer. Jesus validates how privately potent our belief is when he says:

"Everything is possible for one who believes." (Mark 9:23, NIV)

Even though we have such a powerful promise from God we are often drowsy and vague in our expectation.

Maybe we tried prayer at a key moment in the past and our results were meager. Maybe it left us feeling like prayer was more of a Rubik's Cube than an open door to God. For many of us church and prayer have only produced feelings of boredom. We've been worn down by a lifetime of spiritual moments in which we experienced no spiritual power, and our expectation has evaporated. Against that backdrop, however, scripture says, "Without faith it is impossible to please God, because anyone who comes to him must believe that he exists and that he rewards those who earnestly seek him." (Hebrews 11:6 NIV)

We treat belief as if it is a condition handed to us. Like it is done to me instead of built within me. This point of view doesn't stand up under scrutiny. If there was no ability to influence my belief, then why would God hold me accountable for it? Furthermore, if I have no ability to preserve a believing heart then why would God be pleased to find faith in me? If I'm accountable for it and God is pleased with me when I have it, then clearly, I have some contribution to it.

My wife and I grow a modest garden every year. In July the weeds bear down upon us in full force. If we don't push back upon their intrusion, they will take over. We use several methods to deal with the weeds. None are easy and, of course, these are the hottest days of the year. Sweating completely through our clothes is a certainty. Similarly, unbelief will grow in the garden of my life with God. Prayer is the place where I weed out unbelief one rootlet at a time. Like my real garden, weeding out unbelief is work. It's highly intentional and demands that I do more than skim the surface. In the course of time, the atmosphere of faith increases in my soul. To stay the course to the end I will have to weed out unbelief and learn to keep expectation alive.

Disillusionment

When we are honest, every molecule in our body is telling us that we were made for sacred purpose. But sometimes all we can muster is a threadbare spiritual existence. In this disequilibrium prayer feels like it was meant for somebody else, like it works in another time zone but not the one where we are. Once upon a time we felt more idealistic about our life but now disillusionment is a steady source of resistance against my prayers.

Scripture is full of moments when people who trust God hit seasons of disillusion. Like Asaph in Psalm 77:
Will the Lord reject forever? Will he never show his favor again?
Has his unfailing love vanished forever? Has his promise failed
for all time?

Every week at church, I stretch my hands out to pray over people who have come forward to ask for prayer. I let them talk and I listen. I train my inward senses to hear the Holy Spirit's compassion and direction for them. Ultimately, I ask them, "What do you want the Lord to do for you today?" They often grapple to put words to it. In most cases, they are caught in a current of disillusionment. My role is to help them break out of the lies of disillusionment that have rooted down over the days and weeks. I am there to pray for breakthroughs but also to remind them that the way is forward. God's faithfulness awaits those who don't give up and continue forward.

Distraction, disappointment, disbelief, disillusion: they are all formidable sources of breakdown, but let's take it down to its simplest terms. When these seasons come for a visit, I will either default to spiritual distance with God or spiritual grit toward God. This default is my choice.

It is the fulcrum upon which my prayer momentum sways one way or the other.

Much like the last chapter on rhythm, this is about the practical engagement of day after day, month after month, year on top of year, until a lifetime is built. It's not sexy. It's not new, but it is nevertheless vital. I don't change the oil and put gas in my car because it's a new revelation. I do it because the car can't continue forward if I neglect these life-long basics. Not everything in our spiritual economy is inspiring. In thread-bare seasons I need to be instructed and empowered more than I need to be inspired.

Spiritual Grit

Your prayer movement requires grit and personal resolve. But doesn't everything worthwhile in life? Like fitness, like a good marriage, like real friendships, like car maintenance, like home ownership, like a productive garden. Everything worthwhile in life is an uphill hike. A life of prayer is a worship hike. Spiritual grit will be required.

In the long lines of life, losing focus is a downhill situation —it's easy. The pull upon our soul is always toward the new and entertaining. The journey inward through prayer is a perpetual hike. I don't mean to make it sound like drudgery; it is not. In fact, it is a relational hike that yields glorious views that are satisfying. It yields experiences with God that are rewarding. However, the lines of life are long, and the resistance of the uphill climb is always there. It is predictable that we will lose momentum. If the drift of that season is not self-arrested, the drift can become the new norm. Your worship hike could come to a standstill. At that point the fulcrum of life begins to tilt in the direction of distance with God. If this slipping continues, then life begins the long descent into coming apart at the seams.

I realize that offering spiritual grit as the remedy for a hard season is like saying "just try harder". But trying harder is a different mindset than the one that just says, "stay the course." Staying the course simply means I won't give up. It means that while I may adjust in my pursuit of God, the most important choice is the resolve to keep going.

Make it personal

You've heard it quoted in the movies when somebody does harm in the name of progress— "It's not personal, it's strictly business." Your prayer movement will sustain through every season if it is the opposite of this statement. It's never business but always personal.

The pursuit of God is not a thing I do, it's a person that I'm chasing to know. It is possible to do religious discipline without any personal engagement. It is possible to read scripture and recite prayers toward God without budging my heart from its fixed position behind the thorny hedge called 'self.' I'm familiar with the counterfeit moments when my heart is only slightly engaged —like someone who sits politely and stares vacant in a conversation.

Remember the secret of prayer from chapter two: *Prayer is not about prayer; it is about God's presence.* My heart and mind must come together for authentic personal engagement. Nothing else will do.

Distraction, disbelief, disappointment, disillusionment, and all their cousins steal my resolve for authentic heart engagement. But no short-cut exists, I must find the necessary humility to open my shut-up heart once again. When I do, I receive fresh wind in my sails to move forward.

If I've lived a long season of being closed off to God, opening the door may sting at first. But just like a wound that needs cleaning— the cleaning comes before the healing. It hurts but it's necessary. Open your heart, make it personal, and you will begin to close the distance.

Daily Surrender

The surrender of my will has never happened accidentally— it is always intentional. Like the athlete in training who surrenders to the daily rigors of his chosen sport, I must confront my own ego. I must stand up to the inward protest of my soul and learn to bow as a daily habit. Just like the athlete who learns to overcome the resistance he feels in repeated training. The spiritual momentum of my relationship with God learns how to power past the resistance.

Be careful of the slow drift away from the uphill climb. Beware of drifting from the everyday commitment required. Every athlete knows what it's like to stop getting better and to start coasting. They know what it's like to give a half-hearted effort. The DNA testing of prayer has been done— coasting and casual are not there.

Jesus modeled the proper DNA when he made his own hike, carrying the cross up Calvary's hill. One foot in front of the other until he reached the summit. He accomplished redemption for us all. Now we are invited to make our own worship hike and use the redemption pattern of Jesus as our trailhead. When prayer breaks down, go back to the basics, and remember that personal engagement and daily surrender are like a good pair of worship boots —they will keep you ascending the mountain of God. Spiritual grit will be required.

Embrace the Distance
Adopt a distance mindset from the very outset.
Things that go the distance have a beauty of their own. A marathon runner as she crosses the finish line, a marriage that lasts 60 plus years, a life-long friendship, a car that goes over 300,000 miles – whatever it is, we feel impressed, if not inspired.

But distance requires a mindset. I remember a conversation with a friend of mine who had just gotten out of the Marines. He was telling me about his mindset when he was required to do long distance runs in full gear. He said, "You'd be surprised at what you can do when you just keep going. You don't think about the end, you just keep your legs moving." This is not a secret hack; it is a mindset that is embraced. Your life with God is built for longevity. It's not a casual stroll. It is a hike built for the duration of your life. A distance mentality builds resolve.

Just as Jesus worked on his mindset, so we are to work on ours:

> "For the joy set before him he endured the cross, scorning its shame, and sat down at the right hand of the throne of God. Consider him who endured such opposition from sinners, so that you will not grow weary and lose heart." (Hebrews 12:2, NIV)

Make up your mind at the start to see it through to the end and embrace the distance.

Slow and Steady Speed

Everybody is in awe of start-up companies that have meteoric success. They launch an idea and seemingly in no time at all they are billionaires. Like Twitter, a social media idea that launched and hit a valuation of one billion in just twenty-eight months or like the more recent success of Slack, a business communication app that pulled off the same billion-dollar feat in just fifteen months.[34]

We all marvel at these success stories because we understand that life doesn't normally work like this. Success is usually built on the back of patient industry. Even those who have good ideas normally have to show up for work for decades before they can see even a fraction of that kind of success. The normal speed of success is slow and steady. This is the proper mindset for a life-long investment with God.

If you were going to take an actual long-distance hike, you would train. You would start slow and add increased challenges as you drew closer to the day of your hike. Similarly, in prayer, start with doable and honest movements. If they seem embarrassingly meager, you don't have to tell anyone. Just start, and then add length and depth as you go. Remember that most relationships work exactly like this. They begin with moderate commitments of time and effort. As the relationship gains importance, investment increases. This is normal.

Consequently, when I am trying to get back spiritual momentum, I return to the basics. Slow and steady is a mind-set that keeps me from putting too much pressure on myself. Like Denzel Washington said in <u>Remember the Titans,</u> "It's like Novocain, just give it time and it always works."

Innovate the Connection

Don't be surprised when the thing that used to bring you near to God doesn't seem to work anymore. It's normal. The law of diminishing returns states that benefits gained from something at one point in time will yield smaller gains over time even though more energy is invested into it. Typically, this law is used to explain economic cycles, but it is relevant to relationship momentum as well.

My daughter Annie and her husband Rudy are an energetic pair. When they walk in the room the energy and the fun factor increases exponentially. In their dating years they made a habit of well-researched dates. Evenings out at nice restaurants hand-picked. The expectation was high and so was the price. But it was worth the investment. They enjoyed the anticipation, the travel to downtown Atlanta, the conversation over an expensive meal. When they eventually got married, the experiences and the cost began to put too much pressure on their dates. She told me that they ended up getting in arguments every time. What worked so well at producing connection in the past, now was creating distance. So they pivoted away from the pressure of the special experience and decided to go in a completely different direction. They still prioritized time together but now over chicken wings at a place just down the street. They rekindled their dinner date connection by innovating their chosen method. No more arguments, goodbye to pressure, and the return of vital conversation together.

When prayer feels stuck in a diminishing returns cycle, try something different. Like long distance hikers who listen to their bodies and adjust as the hike wears on, our prayer methods need to pivot when they are not leading us as close to God as we want to be. I'm not saying that you should completely abandon something tried and true, but sometimes relationships need to hit the refresh button. They need someone to care enough to try something new. You may find that you can soon return to your former rhythms with a rekindled spirit.

Community

You don't have to hike alone. Nobody does. In fact, it is not recommended. Surround yourself with people who aspire to have an authentic life with God and stick by them. In the thin seasons they will help you continue forward. Our spiritual enemy is an expert in his field, but he is not particularly original. He has one fundamental strategy to ruin you. His method is divide and conquer. His goal is to steal from you, kill you, and destroy the ones you love. But he begins simple— he devises schemes to get you alone. Once he has you alone, he gives you a steady diet of lying thoughts. Without a community to help keep your thoughts tested, you are a prime target for evil intentions.

Think back to some of your hardest seasons and remember that you were tempted to isolate yourself. Maybe your distance from your community turned into distance with God? My experience has been that we tend to create distance with God after we have allowed distance with our community. Or we create distance with our community because we have allowed distance with God. The thin seasons in our spiritual hike require friends who will be there in the dark night and be a voice of encouragement until morning comes.

If you have drifted from your group of trusted friends, put them back into your life as quickly as you can. Not the friends who cause you to drift, but the friends who know God and are cheering you on in your pursuit of Him. The presence of God is a team sport. When His voice gets quiet in private, remember that His ways can still be upheld inside of the community. Keep moving forward together.

When Prayer feels like a dead end

Sometimes disillusionment is not just with life's circumstance, but specifically with prayer. Results in prayer have been so lackluster that they feel non-existent. This can push us to the edge of giving up. This is the story of many, perhaps you.

A few weeks ago, I prayed for a middle-aged husband with a wife and two children. He'd contracted COVID. Because of the hospital restrictions, we could not pray with him in person, so we prayed from a distance. He got better and hope flowed, then he relapsed. This morning I received the news he died.

Many people I've prayed for didn't recover. People die. I know that. But this one came with a particular force of devastation. I turned my heart toward heaven and insisted, "What is that?" That's the best I could muster. "Do these prayers really matter?" No disrespect was directed at heaven, but I didn't hide the weakness of my resolve. I waited only a moment and sensed God's directive. It was simple and strangely comforting.

"Always pray and never give up."

How many times have I read this simple prescription from Jesus? I've taught it to others. But in the middle of disillusionment all the simple answers can seem false. Fortunately for me, God's invitation forward was enough for me. I whispered,

"Ok, I won't."

That seems too simple, doesn't it? Can you really dismantle disillusionment with such a thin conviction? When the voice of the Lord seems like a barely distant echo, I must endure till the sun goes down. Refuse to be taken out. Turn my honest face to God and refuse to draw a line in the dirt that says, "I won't go any farther."

I remember listening to an interview with Olivia Harrison, the wife of former Beatle George Harrison. They were married for twenty-three years before George's death in 2001. In this interview she was asked how she endured through the marriage with multiple episodes of unfaithfulness by her former husband. Her answer was razor quick. She didn't pull something heady out of the clouds, she simply said, "You don't divorce."[35]

I'm not here to debate the merits of her stance. I just want to point to how simple her answer was to the disillusionment that she certainly felt. You stare it in the face, and you make an honest decision to keep moving forward. Thankfully, unlike humans, God is always faithful. In due time you will experience a breakthrough if you do not give up.

God has given us a powerful word to use against the schemes of Satan: "No."
Simple, powerful, noble. It is a tool of supernatural proportions.
"No, I will not settle for this wasteland season."
"No, I will not believe God has abandoned me."
"No, I do not accept the lie that my prayers are futile."

As the scriptures promise: "Let us press on to know the Lord. His going forth is as certain as the dawn. He will come to us like the evening rain." (Hosea 6, NIV)

Or even the more concrete:
"For everyone who asks receives; the one who seeks finds; and to the one who knocks, the door will be opened." (Mat. 7, NIV)
When I feel like prayer has turned into a dead end, I reckon upon the future certainty of these promises and a better day. I continue forward.

Begin Again

Lastly, a word of advice to the one who feels like you've already given up. If all of my encouragement to not give up feels too late for you – then let me tell you how simple it is to get back on course. Begin again.

A friend of mine who was part of the worship team that I was leading unexpectedly showed up at my door. He was pale and jittery. Something was wrong. It took him a few minutes to get to the reason for his visit. He trembled with fear of rejection as he confessed that he had an addiction to porn. He was deeply afraid that I would think less of him. It's been almost twenty years, but I remember it like it was yesterday. All I felt was compassion for him. The first words from my mouth were so healing for him that he reminds me of it to this day. I said, "The road to forgiveness is a short one." He knew that my love for him was fully intact. The only thing that remained was for him to forgive himself and start over with Jesus. Begin again.

If there is distance between you and God, The road is shorter than you think. Begin again. If you have a story of breakdown, it doesn't matter if it's been one day or fifty years, the answer is the same —begin again.

Those who want to see the beauty of the finish line have to learn to begin again.

Invocation

Next Step:
Confront your breakdowns and never give up.

Scripture:
Even though I walk through the valley of the shadow of death, I will fear no evil, for you are with me (Psalm 23:4)

Quote:
You don't possess endurance, you practice it. (Pastor Kevin Myers)

Everything worthwhile in life is uphill, and the only way you go uphill is intentional.
(John Maxwell <u>Intentional Living</u>).

This hill, though high, I covet to ascend; the difficulty will not me offend. For I perceive the way to life lies here. Come, pluck up, heart; let's neither faint nor fear. Better, though difficult, the right way to go, than wrong, though easy, where the end is woe. (John Bunyan, <u>the Pilgrim's Progress</u>)

Prayer:

Repair me, Lord. Lead me back to wholeness. Step into the distance I feel and restore me. I empty my hands; I lay down the distractions that pull upon me. I breathe in my best belief so that you are free to move within me. Wrap my disillusionment in bandages of grace. It is I who have drifted from our relationship, not you. I humbly return. Meet me. Heal me. Help me to daily surrender to your presence over my life.

Chapter 7
THE JOURNEY OF MATURITY

Relationships are made to mature. If they don't mature, they won't endure. It's that simple. Maturity in a relationship is necessary because it's the journey that brings clarity. It's what helps me see my role in the relationship. My sense of responsibility in the relationship increases. But maturity is never guaranteed, meaning it is not automatic. It is a process built upon my willful engagement. One day and then the next. Steadfast and patiently engaged. As my relationship with God matures, the experiences that transpire in prayer mature as well. What does that look like?

Maturity begins with Closeness that builds Trust

In the early days of learning God's presence, my experiences with him were like a quilt pieced together by his closeness. His goodness drawing near and bringing hope to my thread-bare insecurities. The fears and doubts were of a teenage variety, but they were nevertheless real to me. His goodness would draw near and like the perfume from the torch of the ghost of Christmas present in Dickens "*Christmas Carol*", he hovered over me, just to graciously pour himself upon my uncertainties. In small measure at first, and then more as I became more aware. Like a beautiful song being whispered, as I became familiar with the melody, I could follow it better. Pure but not demanding. He was there for me. The only request he seemed to be making was for me to notice and receive his presence. He gently brought his person to me for my good.

Isn't this how undeniable trust is built? Isn't this how mothers etch out an irreplaceable position in our hearts? They give from a place of unconditional affection. When we are infants, they have all the comfort, all the resources, all protection and they give it without expectation of repayment. In doing so they reflect God. He loves without condition and teaches me the language of his longing. Remarkably, it's me. I am in the center of his affection, and it marks me.

When I was in high school there was a fifteen-minute break at 10am between classes. Like most 10th graders, I enjoyed hanging out with my friends in the hallway. Sometime that year I decided to give those fifteen minutes to God. I slipped away quietly to the backside of one of the buildings on campus and just sat on the ground with my back against the brick wall and lingered with him. No radical encounters of God's presence happened, but I was aware of his pleasure at my decision to be with him. I was not alone. I was learning that if I would simply set aside time and space, he would meet me.

Little was required of me at this stage. The relationship was in its infancy. Beautiful in simplicity, but immature. But that was just the start. Trust was being established. Like a garden seed planted in good ground, the outer defenses of my soul soon broke open. The transformation that maturity brings must walk through the death of my solitary existence. As I learn to trust that he is there, a higher vision for my life settles upon me — the vision of a life with God.

Maturity moves from Independence to Dependence

It is my stubborn independence that gets me in trouble. It is my misguided instinct to go it alone that steers me into a spiritual ditch. This independent "me" kingdom hides. It wears shades of gray and complains about its own way, unsatisfied.

Selfish discontent is the tendency of my soul, but I've learned that I can be anchored through time spent with God. However, the privilege of his presence requires a posture of dependence. It requires a humbling of my outward shell. This humbling is unnatural to me. Somewhere deep down every molecule in me resists the capitulation required. What a strange predicament this produces. The One who is the source of my greatest comfort is the One I so easily resist. The One who builds my trust with His nearness now seems to come with a cover charge. Without question, the cover charge isn't coming from Him. It's rooted in me. I am like the immature puppy who wants the treat in the master's hand but is reticent to get close enough for the transaction. Slowly, through repeated training the puppy dispels his fear and learns to depend upon his master. That's me in prayer.

In the course of time, I learned that dependence upon God is superior in every way to my natural instincts of self-rule. Like the seed buried in good ground, though the outward shell had to break, something new and ripe with potential was beginning to bloom.

Reactive prayer matures into Proactive prayer
Maybe you are like me. I began my prayer pursuit of God in a reactive mode. Reactive prayers are prayers shaped around my desire to escape life circumstances. Something has gone awry, I'm in pain and so I turn to God for a rescue – it is a cry for help.

Reactive prayer, of course, makes sense, and for the duration of our life it will always be permissible and intelligent to cry out to God when we are in trouble. However, we often get in trouble because we fail to be proactive in our relationship with God. We get casual first and then we get careless, and this leads to trouble. When trials come, we cry out to God. But maturity in prayer means that we learn how to navigate through trouble by being proactive.

The great privilege of prayer is that we are invited to process life before the breakdowns occur. Proactive conversations are almost always superior to reactive ones. Rather than just reacting to problems, I learn to address the core issues that cause the problems. Rather than trying to quell desperation, I'm stockpiling peace. Rather than being undone by my unmet expectations, I'm shaping my desires around God's Kingdom. Proactive prayer is the path for keeping trouble from developing into a full-on breakdown. It is the way for processing problems before a life avalanche occurs.

My friend, Pastor Kevin Myers, woke up in the middle of the night and being wide awake decided to get up and pray. He walked quietly to the bedroom door of his teenage daughter. A wedge had begun in their relationship. They'd always enjoyed being close, but in this season something was off. The problem? He'd given her a puppy AND they'd just moved into a new house. The puppy had not yet learned the rules of where to poop and pee. A few accidents happened and it was putting distance between them.

Even though he had no desire for a puppy, his love for his daughter conquered his inward objections. He wanted her to have the desire of her heart. Consequently, he laid down his preference to not have a puppy so that he could delight the heart of his daughter. She was thrilled. But now, all of this was at risk because of his frustration. He was putting pressure on her to keep a closer eye on the puppy's potty habits. But now, as he stood at his daughter's door in the middle of the night, the Holy Spirit turned the conversation in his direction and warned him to change his disposition. "You are driving your daughter away. You need to lighten up and learn to love what she loves. If you do not heed this word, you will continue to drive a wedge in your relationship with her and you will regret it." His proactive prayers helped him resolve the trouble with his daughter before it turned into a breakdown. God gave him insider information about what was going on in her heart. He listened and adjusted, and only God knows how much trouble was avoided because there was a father praying in the middle of the night. Maturity learns the advantage of proactive prayers and prays accordingly.

Maturity progresses through Familiarity to Affection

The steady investment of prayer conversations with God taught me familiarity with God. I understand if this seems slightly offensive, for who should ever claim familiarity with The Living God. It sounds too casual. However, by familiar I don't mean casual. And I certainly don't mean the bored familiarity of the married couple sitting at the restaurant at a table for two, both of them scrolling their phones. Tragic. No, I mean that God keeps himself in the lane of personality and he can be known in ways like what we would call friendship.

His affections can be felt. His preferences discerned, his voice learned. His mirth detected. Always supported by scripture but nevertheless colored by experience. As my familiarity with God broadens, my affection for him deepens. Slowly he places his mark deep in my soul, and I am ruined for all other cheap gods or earthly imitations.

God marked me when I was still in college. While I was at home on a school break, I went out into the night air to take a walk and talk to God. I was processing in prayer— brooding in my thoughts about the direction of my life. I was telling God about the many unmet desires in my soul. Then, as I walked through a wooded pasture, I was suddenly aware of God asking me a direct question. I didn't hear a voice with my outward ears, but the question was articulate, specific and direct. He asked, "What is success to you?"

It was a holy moment. It seemed like God asked the question but also gave me the answer, for without any hesitation, I answered, "Success is knowing you, hearing your voice and telling others what you've said."

Those words flowed out effortlessly though I'd never said them before. That was my answer, and I immediately felt the pleasure of God. My answer pleased him.

My life has been on a different trajectory since that moment. He is the treasure, his voice my delight, his ways my path. The arc of maturity works this way. It treasures the relationship more than the benefits that come from the relationship. In the beginning I was delighted by what I got from God, but through time and maturity the delight becomes knowing God himself.

Maturity embraces Shared Purpose with God

Important relationships always mature into shared purpose. In marriage you are building a life together. In business you are working to provide a profitable way of life, making money for yourself and others, perhaps creating meaning and purpose through patient industry. In friendship you are building a way to share your life with others: to laugh, pursue hobbies, create memories, and have important conversations. Whatever the relationship, as it matures, there is a point when you realize you are building something together. This is what I mean by shared purpose.

So, likewise, as prayer matures it leads us into shared purpose with God. I am no longer there only to enjoy the relationship, but also to embrace a shared sacred mission. When this sense of shared purpose develops, it empowers me differently. My desires begin to take shape around God's interests. His purposes have become my purpose. It changes the whole tone of my life, consequently, the inner workings of my conversations with God change as well.

My life becomes a supervisor of sacred purpose. God is building his Kingdom and I am a co-laborer. I am much less of an observer enjoying the view from God's train and more of a cabin steward of the box cars he has put in my trust. Attending to the needs of others and contending for heaven's outcomes upon earth. The prayer of shared purpose is the one Jesus gave us — "Your Kingdom come, your will be done, on earth as it is in heaven."

I am not just looking for a better life for myself; I am keeping watch over every place where I carry responsibility, prayerfully asking that the outcomes in those places would be an expression of God's plan and purpose. I pray that situations surrounding my soul, my family, my work, my church, my nation would be shaped according to his will. Not some vague picture of God's will but my best understanding of "on earth as it is in heaven."

Maturity clarifies Identity

As I mature in my relationship with God, he slowly dismantles the false identities that I have constructed and leads me to see myself correctly. We all tend to have lies that we have believed about ourselves. The lies are usually seeded into our souls by seasons of trauma, abuse, repeated lies spoken over us, bullying, or any number of debilitating insecurities. False identities are constructs that the devil and his forces use to assist us in under-living our lives. God has buried greatness in each of us, but the lie of false identity conspires hard against us finding and living out that greatness.

God uses prayer to chip away at the lies. One by one he peels them from our identity. Meanwhile, like a beautiful song in the background whose volume is slowly ever increasing, the desires that God places within us come to the surface. They become purified in the cleansing effect of his presence. These core desires are the building blocks of our true self. God is not trying to quash our desires. He is awakening desire, shaping, purifying, and calling us to take steps. It is like the chair seated by the fire where our Father invites conversation that helps us understand ourselves. In this discovery, I feel seen, understood, known, and commissioned.

Jesus said about prayer, "Your Father knows what you need before you ask him." (Matthew 6:8, ESV) The effective way to arrive at your identity is to ask your heavenly Father. "Who am I? Show me what I need to know about myself? How do you want to use the desire that lives in me?"

Responding to the Resolute Love of God

I connected with a friend of mine yesterday. He is a worship pastor and a favorite of everyone who knows him. We were catching up with each other, filling in the gaps for the last eight months. He began to tell me of a crisis season he walked through. His father died and some radical changes had taken place with his job at his church. He began to doubt his faith. Profound feelings of imbalance between his outward role and his inward reality paralyzed his life. He is a naturally genuine person, so the dissonance was destroying him. Hopelessness invaded his soul. He wanted to quit his job. He wanted to quit life.

Then he encountered Jesus in prayer.

He'd become so lost in his thoughts and feelings that he broke open in adamant protest to God. Speaking to heaven sternly, authentic, and untethered to any formalities. He wept openly, raised his voice, and began to build his case of unbelief.

Then Jesus spoke: "Yes, but I love you."

Once wasn't enough to assuage his wrestling, so he continued his attack and poured out more objections. Then he heard it again, "Yes, but I love you." I sat entranced in this story as he related how everything began to shift under the adamant confession of God's love toward him. God was pulling him out of the pit that ensnared him. Freedom rolled in like a weather front from a different land. He capped his story by saying, "I've never seen it this way before, but I think **God's love is violent.**"

As soon as he said it, I felt like I knew what he meant, but I asked him to elaborate and he said, "It felt like heaven was coming down upon me to break me out of the prison that I had built. Much like if my son was in trouble behind a locked door, I would break my way through to get to him. It was God's unrelenting stubbornness to say the healing words

'Yes, but I love you,' over every barrier that I had built. It was a love rescue so insistent that it went way beyond polite."

Don't we all long for this kind of love?

Persistent, undaunted, adamant, active, fierce, extreme, and unbridled – a love that defeats every objection? I want that for my life. I want to be loved like that. I want a God who loves me violently, passionately, and protectively. Like the father in Luke 15 with the prodigal son. The father only needed to see his son returning from a distance and he ran to meet him. He fell upon his neck and kissed him. He commanded his servants, "Hurry and bring the best robe and put it on my son. Put a ring on his finger and shoes on his feet. Prepare the fatted calf for tonight we will celebrate!"

God's love is a contending love— meaning it is unwilling to settle into lukewarm. Ready to fight for me, willing to wrestle with me, unwilling to be passive.

God's contending love for me is the foundation for a life of contending devotion to him. Slow down and read that sentence again —the idea of contending prayer dominates the rest of this book. We must understand prayer from this posture. The foundation for contending prayer is this— God deserves a response from me that is as unbridled, unequivocal, and unembarrassed as his love is for me. I can never pay God back for what He's done for me, but I can respond to him in like kind. **Beyond politeness. Insistent. Sacrifice for sacrifice. Love for love.** This is the posture of shared purpose. I am no longer just working on my relationship with God; I am partnering with him in a co-laboring dynamic to see things accomplished on earth. But the atmosphere of this response is not obligation or duty. It is insistent, sacrificial, and responding love.

Love contends

For many this word *contend* conveys a negative undertone. It carries an adversarial flavor because it essentially means to fight, to wrestle, to strive or struggle. But it fits, for in prayer we hit every single angle of the word. If we open our eyes as we read scripture, we will not only find contending to be a common posture of people who walked with God, but we also see that God prefers and sometimes requires it.

Abraham negotiates with God over the city of Sodom. Jacob wrestles with the Angel of God unwilling to let go until he receives a blessing. Moses debates with God, reminding God that he has a reputation to defend. Gideon grapples with God to get a sign to assuage his fear. Jeremiah complains. Job all but puts God on trial. God looked on each one with favor and used them to accomplish his purpose. This boldness with God does not mean arrogance or pride. No, God resists such things. However, He regards the kindly, the lowly, the meek, the humble, the trusting; but none of these exclude the courageous boldness that God seems to like.

Mary, the mother of Jesus, is famously regarded as meek and humble, and yet, she also questioned the angel's declaration of pregnancy, understandably asking him to elaborate and give her more clarity. Later, just before Jesus entered his public ministry, she pressured him to turn water into wine.

Are we any different?

Don't we prefer an active, participatory, deeply engaged opinion on the other side of our relationships? A lack of boldness in the relationship suggests the lack of care. Casual non-engagement is offensive. Contending is the absence of boredom. It is supported by the character of engagement captured by the Yiddish word *"chutzpah."* It means self-confidence, audacity, and boldness – present and accounted for.

Jesus later taught his disciples:
In a certain city there was a judge who neither feared God nor respected man. And there was a widow in that city who kept coming to him saying, 'Give me justice against my adversary.' For a while he refused, but afterward he said to himself, 'Though I neither fear God nor respect man, yet because this widow keeps bothering me, I will give her justice, so that she will not beat me down by her continual coming . . . will not God give justice to his elect, who cry to him day and night? Will he delay long over them? I tell you he will give justice to them speedily. (Luke 18)

We think of this parable as being about perseverance in prayer, and it is. However, it is also about bold courage. The widow in the story was persistent but she also was brave. She thought large and did not shrink back before the one who could help her.

The story is one of contrast. God is not the unrighteous judge. He is in juxtaposition with the unrighteous judge. The judge's heart is slow to move and begrudging. God's heart is to move speedily. The posture of the one asking is the point – it is a persevering and contending posture, and this is how Jesus says we should pray.

When Jesus taught his disciples to pray, he gave them the Lord's Prayer. The centerpiece of that prayer is "Your Kingdom come; your will be done on earth as it is in heaven." What we miss when we read this in English is the fact that it is not a question, it is not a request, it is an imperative statement. Jesus is inviting us to require the Kingdom of heaven in the present moment. Strange to our sensibilities, we are instructed to insist with contending boldness that heaven influences earth.

In a similar fashion, Jesus makes the odd request for us to pray that God would send workers into the harvest. He said, "The harvest is plentiful, but the laborers are few: therefore, **pray earnestly** [contend] to the Lord of the harvest to send out laborers into his harvest." (Matthew 9:37-38 NIV) Doesn't it strike you as odd that Jesus would prescribe earnest prayer for the sending out of workers? Why doesn't God just send the workers himself? This is a great question and one that points to the fact that God has made himself responsive to our co-laboring prayers. Contending boldness required.

If the posture of contending seems outside the bounds of a healthy relational dynamic, then think of it as watchfulness. Not contending WITH the one who is loved but contending FOR the one who is loved. In this light, contending is not a special breed of prayer but the normal and ongoing posture of prayer.

I was not trained to pray this way. Neither was I taught to view prayer in a co-laboring paradigm. Prayer seemed more like a way to get a little boost from heaven in a self-help system. But it turns out that prayer is more of a war-time commission, an exit ramp from my personal empire and an on-ramp to the expanding government of Jesus. It is a highly charged love story taking place in the middle of a battle. To thrive in this place, I must learn to be watchful— to contend. When I do so, I make my presence known in specific ways.

Force of Opinion

One of my wife's favorite movies is the romantic comedy *While You Were Sleeping*. One of the scenes from that movie makes us laugh. Sandra Bullock's character Lucy is talking to her potential love interest Jack. They are just getting to know each other, and Jack begins to describe a posture in the relationship called "Leaning." He mistakenly thought Lucy was interested in her neighbor (a chubby Italian named Joe Jr.) The conversation went like this:

Jack: It was just a misunderstanding... and on top of the Joe Jr. thing!
Lucy: Excuse me?
Jack: Nothing *(trying to play it off)*
Lucy: No, no, It's not nothing now. What Joe Jr. thing?
Jack: The leaning thing.
Lucy: The leaning thing?
Jack: Yeah.
Lucy: OK . . . um, what do you mean by the "leaning thing?" Because he gave me flowers?
Jack: And then you leaned.

Lucy: And then I leaned... ok. How did I lean when I leaned?

Jack: How were you leaning? It's a lot different than hugging. Hugging is very different. It involves arms and hands. Leaning is whole bodies moving in like this *(he draws near and looks her in the eye)*. Leaning involves wanting and accepting. Leaning... *(and just before the inevitable first kiss, the mood is jolted by the appearance of Joe Jr.)*

Joe Jr.: Hey Luce! Is this guy bothering you?

Lucy: No

Joe Jr.: Are you sure because it looks like he's... leaning?

It's a light chuckle at best. But this idea of "Leaning" is a good way to think of relational force. In romance, leaning is wooing through intimacy. In friendship, it is bold influence through familiarity. In business, leaning is leverage and negotiations for mutually shared purpose. Contending prayer is all the above. It is exerting relational force. It is the desire for an outcome expressed to God with focused attention, willful force, mental resolve, and emotional zeal. It demands that I bring robust opinions and forward longings into prayer. It requires me to filter all the above through humble surrender. But make no mistake, it is this relational force that God seems to love.

Belief

Heaven is on record —God likes faith. It provokes him to act. Jesus championed this preference for belief on multiple occasions. He changed his mind, changed his plan, altered the moment, all in response to faith.

Jesus stops his journey to the centurion's house and decides to instantly heal from a distance in response to the centurion's faith. (Luke 7)

Who can forget the contending boldness of the Canaanite woman who needed deliverance for her daughter? At first Jesus seems to ignore her. But she kept crying out. The disciples became annoyed and asked Jesus to send her away.

Jesus finally addresses her, "I was sent only to the lost sheep of Israel."
She is unwilling to give up, "Lord, Help me!"
Jesus puts a little more force in his resistance, "It is not right to take the children's bread and toss it to the dogs."
She refuses to be offended and uses his own metaphor to demonstrate her resolve. "Yes Lord, but even the dogs eat the crumbs that fall from their master's table."
That one got him! Jesus said, "You have great faith! Your request is granted." (Mat. 15)
Faith takes risks and inevitably achieves its objective or fails in the attempt. But make no mistake, in the economy of God, faith is a provoking stance.

Failure
When prayer seems to fail at its objective, it re-ups and tries again. It looks for another way. It tramples out another path to its objective.
A man came to Jesus and informed him,
"I brought you my son, who is possessed by a spirit . . . I asked your disciples to drive out the spirit, but they could not."

Jesus's response is not one we often quote. In frustration Jesus responds:

"You unbelieving generation, how long shall I stay with you? How long shall I put up with you? Bring the boy to me."

Jesus casts out the spirit and the boy is healed. (Mark 9)

Afterwards, in private, the disciples asked, "Why couldn't we drive it out?" The disciples failed in their attempt but let me point out that they tried. They fought for the desired result and failed. How many of us would have elected to sit this one out? Not the disciples; they stepped up. When they failed, they sought answers. That is my favorite part of the story. The disciples were not content to drop the matter, to accept their failure as the norm. They wanted to see better results in the future. Consequently, they pursued answers from Jesus. Similarly, we must not let our failures cause us to stop contending for better results. Like the disciples, we need to get better answers from Jesus and try again.

Success

Success creates momentum. Each breakthrough enlarges our capacity to believe bigger next time. I love David's response to Goliath's taunts. "Your servant has killed both the lion and the bear; this uncircumcised Philistine will be like one of them, because he has defied the armies of the living God." (1 Samuel 17:36, NIV) David had taken risks before. He had prevailed against the lion and the bear. This uncircumcised Philistine was a notch above them in danger but not to David. His confidence was sky-high. This scene had played out before. Others were passive but David ran toward the giant. You know the end of the story. David separated Goliath's head from his body and raised it up in victory before the end of the day. We are designed by God to grow in our spiritual capacities. Our co-laboring efforts are supposed to yield bigger victories as the years pass by. **Results are not the only thing that matter but they always matter.** When we see them, our confidence soars and we become bolder in prayer.

Contending in Every Direction

John Maxwell's leadership classic *The 360 Degree Leader* teaches that leadership operates in a 360-degree paradigm. He teaches that good leaders influence those above them in their organization. They influence those who are their equal in the organization. And they influence those who are below them. They lead up, lead sideways and lead down. Prayer operates in a 360-degree paradigm as well; for what leadership is to organizational movement, contending prayer is for kingdom progress. It gets things done.

Hands Up Intercession
(Contending up)

In Exodus 17, Moses told Joshua to take soldiers and defeat the Amalekites. Moses pledged to go to the top of the hill overlooking the battle and raise the staff of God. When Moses held up his hands the Israelite army prevailed. When he grew tired and let his arms rest, the Israelites lost ground. The work of keeping Moses' hands raised in prayer was so important that Aaron and Hur came to stand by his side to keep his hands held high. With hands held high, Israel defeated the

Amalekites— a picture of "Hands Up" intercessory prayer. Hands up, of course, doesn't mean that our hands must be raised, but hands up, instead, means that our persistence to be heard on high is built from intentionality, grit, and community.

Moses didn't randomly find himself on that hilltop. He said "no" to other preoccupations to make sure the battle prevailed. Though weariness set in, he applied the necessary grit to maintain his role until the battle was completed. He needed the help of a community to see it through. Contending prayer will always have a solo expression, but it is amplified in community. Moses' arms would have certainly failed without the combined strength of Aaron and Hur. Similarly, our strength to maintain momentum, and our resolve to not give up are made stronger when shared with others.

Every Saturday morning our church gathers to pray over our weekend services –early morning prayer to renew our hearts in God's presence. The attendance is always the minority. It's the remnant who see the value in the inconvenience of gathered prayer. I'll admit that Saturday morning never feels convenient. But let me speak with equal candor and say, it's only inconvenient from the dulled senses of the flesh. Whatever the cost, we always get more in return than we paid out. The interruption of my challenged calendar is nothing compared to a parched spirit that finds a drink. The voices rise like incense to praise, the praise graduates into adamant intercession. Lifting hands to God in a posture of dependence. Churches that pray together prevail; those that do not stall.

Hands On Encounter
(Contending Sideways)

My shared purpose with Jesus includes my reaching out to pray for others like Jesus did. I must stay ready to pray and assist them in encounters with Jesus. We don't defer to some future moment, we pray now.

A girl came forward to our church altar for prayer with her whole family. Five or six of them. She was in pain from scoliosis and wanted healing prayer. As we stood in front of the church, her family stood by watching to see what would happen. She asked to be relieved of the pain. The look on her face was strained. After a few moments of establishing an awareness of God's presence. I looked at her and she looked at me. I made a simple command for her pain to be gone. It was wonderfully immediate. The look on her face shifted into surprise. Something was happening. She leaned over and whispered into the ear of her sister to tell her that the pain disappeared. I asked her if the pain was gone. She smiled the most beautiful smile and nodded "yes." I love the look on people's faces when they have a present-tense encounter with miracle Jesus.

We need a church resolute to pray boldly and to pray right now—stretching out our hands in his name to see broken things restored. This is certainly the model that Jesus gave to us. But it did not stop there; the early church received the commission from Jesus to do what they'd seen him do. Acts 5 says "It happened that the father of Publius lay sick with fever and dysentery. And Paul visited him and prayed, and putting his hands on him, healed him." (Acts 5:16, ESV)

Maturity in prayer cultivates a mindset of readiness. It undergirds its readiness with a biblical understanding. We've been invited to co-labor with the Living God. Too fantastic to believe, but nevertheless true and we are accountable. Our mindset is the Holy Spirit's playground. When we curate a vibrant, expectant mindset, it is like preparing a kitchen for a master chef. He does the work, but we are responsible to be prepared for action.

Outcomes

We do not release ourselves from the desire for results but neither do we tether ourselves to discouragement for any lack of them. We learn to pray again. There is something about praying for someone that is like digging a hole. Each shovel full gets you closer than you were before. **Pray again.**

My friend Jon is a talented musician. He came into rehearsal one day, and I knew when I saw him that he was under the weight of an attack. He'd been suffering awful migraines. When they descended upon him, he could barely function. He was scheduled to do some work in the recording studio and had arrived a few hours early. I could see the discouragement that was sitting over his life. I walked over to him and prayed for God's intervention and commanded the migraine to leave. Nothing. No relief.

This was not the first time I had prayed for this specific problem with Jon. I had prayed at least a dozen times before on different occasions. I'll admit that with the lack of results from my previous prayers I was tempted to turn my prayers for healing into words of empathy and friendship concern. Empathy and concern are always important, but the example of Jesus and the invitation of scripture is to heal.

I told him to go to the studio and I would check on him in an hour. When I circled back, not only was he not better, but he was buried in hopelessness. He said, "I don't have trouble believing that God would heal somebody else, but I just don't think he will for me." He said, "The only thing that has worked are the shots I take, but they are so expensive that I can't take them as often as I need them." He felt trapped

I asked him what the shots do medically. He described what the shot accomplishes. I asked him if I could **pray again.** This time I would simply ask for the power of God to do what these shots were doing. I prayed an unimpressive second prayer. About 45 seconds worth. When I looked up, my friend started acting strange. I asked him, "What's going on?" He said, "I don't know?" But he began to weep and went into a healing encounter with Jesus.

Twenty minutes later he was on cloud nine. All the pain and pressure gone he felt giddy and said he kept getting 'goosebumps.' Not only healed, but better than normal. It marked me. A second prayer. Unimpressive, but enough to open heaven's goodness.

Feet for Trampling
(Contending Down)
Several years ago I awoke in the middle of the night. Sleepy-eyed I looked past my wife sleeping next to me to the open door of our bedroom. Even though the room was dark, I saw a shadowy figure standing

in our doorway. He had no features that I could see, just the outline of a body so dark that I could see his silhouette against the darkness of the house. I knew it wasn't an actual human person like a night-time thief. My reflex thought was that it was a malevolent spirit. But as soon as I had the thought, I doubted. I thought my eyes were playing tricks on me. As this doubt flickered across my mind the figure launched forward toward our bed. With no thought, just pure reflex, I leaned over to cover my wife. Simultaneous to this I heard her react in fear. It rushed toward our bed and then instantly evaporated. Mary Anne, frightened, asked "Did you see that?"

I had no idea that she was even awake until she reacted in fear. I wanted to know what she had seen, so I simply answered, "See what?" She perfectly described the same thing I had seen. I confessed, "I saw it too." We were both a little rattled by the experience.

I was grateful that she saw exactly what I saw so that the experience was validated. We spent a few minutes praying over our room, our bed, our lives. We declared the Lord Jesus as our covering and went back to sleep. My impression of the whole episode was that whatever that demonic figure was, he was there for the purpose of fear. His intent was only to disrupt our peace and enjoy our momentary fright. Perhaps he hoped to plant a seed of fear that would turn the solace of our bedroom into a theater of his ongoing operation. I don't know. What I do know is that once we prayed our peace returned, and he has never appeared again.

We have an enemy: ruthless, heartless, and hateful. He is competent in the art of evil designs against us, and prayer is our primary tool against him.

Paradise Lost is one of my favorite reads. It is an epic telling of the fall of Lucifer from heaven and his evil intentions against Adam and Eve, and through them, the whole race of mankind. As Lucifer comes to terms with his banished state he says,

> "So farewell hope, and with hope, farewell fear, Farewell remorse; all good to me is lost; Evil be thou my good; by thee at least divided empire with heaven's King I hold, By thee, and more than half perhaps will reign; As man ere long, and this new world shall I know."[36]

Perhaps, as this quote suggests, in his mind Satan has nothing else to lose, and in his evil delusions, still half or more to gain. He is the spiritual reality behind layers of suffering and misery. We live in a spiritually contested space. But the outcome of the war is not up for grabs. Jesus has already won. When He pronounced his concluding words from the cross, "It is finished," Satan, perhaps, heard an admission of defeat. But the dark angel assigned the wrong meaning. Just upon the moment of Satan's rejoicing hung his eternal nightmare. Upon the epic moment of Jesus' resurrection from the dead, the tables turned. What Satan thought was a moment of victory was snatched away in pitiful defeat. The war is won but the battle is not over.

All authority in heaven and earth now belongs to glorious King Jesus. In due time every knee will bow. But, until Jesus returns to take his place as the proper king, Earth spins through space as contested territory.

Like a wounded animal, Satan roams looking for someone to devour. He trades in the currency of fear and is desperately wicked. He will be cast down in the end. But for now, he contests the victory of Jesus by deceiving and attacking the dwellers of earth. He cannot save himself, but he can contend for the souls of humanity— the ones deeply loved by God. It is a warfare of vengeance.

Each of us walks into the gospel of Jesus freely. It's our decision. Having made that choice, we are conscripted into spiritual military service. To remain passive on this front is the spiritual equal of being AWOL.

We are compelled by family allegiance and shared purpose to lash out against every vestige of enemy activity. Our weapon is prayer. We contend over lives, over cities, over nations, over our beloved earth with one adamant cry: **your Kingdom come, your will be done on Earth as it is in heaven.** We are watchful against every vestige of life gone wrong. The inward voice of the Holy Spirit says, "an enemy has done this," and we contend for a better outcome—one that is consistent with the heart of Heaven.

God grants trampled ground

Fifteen years ago, my wife came down with a serious colon condition. We went to multiple doctors. They all started out confident but ended up just as defeated as we were. Prayers stacked up, one day after the other, as we waited for heaven's intervention—desperately needing God to break in and be as real as our tears on our cheeks. Nothing seemed to work. Contending prayer in this season was emotionally hard because it was the same prayer day after day, while debilitating symptoms knocked us to the ground.

Two years rolled by. One Friday I was at the church preparing for a service of worship. I went out to pray in the woods beside our church. The prayer trail looked more worn than usual – heavy foot traffic, well-worn and wide. Just like the daily prayers I had been aiming at heaven. Then suddenly with no warning I heard the Lord say, "**God grants trampled ground.**" I didn't hear it out loud, but I heard it. I knew at that moment that Mary Anne was going to be healed.

It took thirty days until we got the news from her doctor confirming what the Lord had promised. "Her colon looks entirely normal," were his exact words. Music to my ears. All the symptoms left, and we got our life back.

I learned from this story that God indeed grants trampled ground. Our feet are made to step on the neck of all the power of the enemy. Sometimes the trampling is a single moment of taking a stand in prayer. But other times it is a journey of continued perseverance. Humble insistence. Wearing out a path to God, knowing that the God of peace will soon crush Satan under my feet.

Sometimes the work of Satan seems to win out when healing doesn't happen, or the breakthrough doesn't arrive. But resolve must not be conquered. Keep marching forward. Let your resilience be heard on high.

Humble Insistence

Humility is the quality of realizing that I am a servant. I don't stand on my own; I am in the service of a King. However, it is the strangest turn in the story that the King would require my insistence to see his will accomplished. But that is exactly our circumstance. How many battles remain unconquered because we have no insistence with God? Perhaps our answers to prayer seem vague and half-done because our insistence is undercooked.

We make the mistake of presiding over our prayers with the same posture with which we received our salvation. Completely bankrupt we said yes to Jesus in salvation. The only thing we bring to the table in salvation is the sin that makes it so necessary. However, our regeneration through Jesus changed our stars. Inside of our salvation through Jesus, our identity goes from a sinner separated from the voice of God to an elevated place in God's economy. We struggle with this shift. God does not. He bought and paid for it. We are like beggars who inherited a fortune but never acclimated to our new station. We pray quietly and small because the beggar in us cannot believe that we've been invited into the castle dining room.

The 17th century English poet, John Donne wrote this same thought: "Thou hadst nothing to do in the first work of thy regeneration; thou couldst not so much as wish it; but in all the rest, thou art a fellow-worker with God"[37]

Peter Grieg writes,

"Jesus models a mystical militancy: wrestling with the devil in the wilderness, rejoicing as he sees Satan fall from heaven, shouting his rebuke to the storm, casting demonic spirits into the abyss. He might well be viewed as a little extreme by many of his churches today. Contemplative prayer and quiet conversation with God may not always be enough. If we truly want to see the kingdom of God return to the enemy-occupied world, we cannot avoid a certain aggression in prayer any more than a soldier can avoid his gun, or a boxer his fists."[38]

I am by nature prone to hand God the football on the 20-yard line and ask him to run the ball for an 80-yard touchdown. I promise that when he crosses the goal line that I will be there to celebrate. But in God's design, he hands the ball back to me and says,

"I'll call the plays. You just say "Yes" and run the ball. The Holy Spirit will do the blocking."

I'm not confused. It's his power, his authority, his presence that wins the day, but he has decreed that my wholehearted participation is central to scoring touchdowns. Prayer is for relationship, however, inside of the relationship, I've been given the responsibility to carry a Holy Spirit guided protest for the will of God to be done on Earth as it is done in heaven.

Sovereignty

Lastly, you may ask, "Doesn't a posture of contending ignore the fact that God is sovereign?" To the profound weight of this question, let me draw a simple picture. When I was a child, I was aware that my parents held all the knowledge and power, but it did not keep me from leaning upon that knowledge and power with the full extent of my desire. I trusted them completely, but I nevertheless maneuvered my voice to be heard by them. In keeping to the wise way of my 5-year-old self, let God be sovereign and yet hear the full force of my request. Any concern that I have about praying in the opposite direction of God's sovereign plan is perhaps sincere, but in the end, it is energy wasted.

Caleb Spirit

You remember the story. God commissioned that a group of spies be sent out to Canaan as a pre-invasion measure. From the beginning, God had promised to give them the land.

"Send some men to explore the land of Canaan, which I am giving to the Israelites." (Numbers 13) He didn't say "might give," he didn't say "maybe." God did not send spies to determine IF Israel should take Canaan. He gave them the command to spy it out to fulfill their co-laboring role. He wasn't planning to do this FOR them; He was promising to do this THROUGH them. God never hesitated in his promise to give them victory. As you probably know from the story, twelve spies were sent out but only two believed that God's promise of victory was enough to win the day. The majority vote of the spies was rooted in fear. It was rooted in the forgetfulness of who they were, of who had sent them. Maturity in prayer develops a Caleb spirit.

Caleb kept it simple. Fully aware that he was walking on enemy contested ground, he resolved his prayer posture like this: **"We should go**

up and take possession of the land for we can certainly do it!" He was not flippantly hyping up the crowd. He reduced all his fears, all his unanswerable questions, down to rest upon what God had promised and commanded. What was true for Caleb in physical reality is true for us in spiritual reality. Our victory is rooted in what God has declared to us, but a faith-filled, co-laboring stance is still required.

Convenience

Can you imagine that Caleb's bold stance played out conveniently for him? No, the peer pressure to conform feels costly. The decision to go to war instead of diverting to the uncontested desert is costly. War is always costly. Yes, our war is in the unseen realm of prayer but make no mistake, it is costly. We must remember that love is measured by its cost. It's intentional, built with grit, sweat, and inconvenience.

We live in a culture that is in love with convenience. We must wake up and see that convenience steals the power of demonstrated love. If following Jesus in co-laboring prayer feels costly and inconvenient, then you know you are treading the sacred sod of demonstrated love. The will of God is not a secret; it's just costly. Bring heaven into focus and then pray, "On earth as it is in heaven." Boldly contend for your desired outcome until you achieve the matter or temporarily fail. Either way, remember, you are talking to God. Anything is possible.

Invocation

Next Step:
Embrace the journey of maturity and take the purposes of God as your own.

Scripture:
And will not God bring about justice for his chosen ones, who cry out to him day and night? (Luke 18:7).

I will indeed do what you have asked, for you have found favor with me, and you are my friend.
(Exodus 33:17)

Quote:
We prevail with men by impudence because they are displeased with it, but with God because he is pleased with it.
Matthew Henry

Let's not settle for polite prayers that bore us and change nothing.
Ray Ortlund

Prayer:

Father touch my spiritual eyes so that I may see the heights to which you've called me. I want to lay down the hesitancy that pulls me toward smaller versions of my life. You always make more of me; you call me higher. I give you my yes. I contend for your purposes. Thank you for including me. I praise you, for you are a Father who insists upon my joy, my desires, my participation. Today I present myself before you as a living sacrifice. I delight in you and proclaim your victory over every square inch of this earth.

Chapter 8
Everybody

A few years ago, as I was leading an evening service of prayer, the Holy Spirit impressed a picture into my thoughts. I was on stage before the congregation. It felt as if I was seeing the crowd with spiritual eyes. It was a flash moment where it seemed like I saw the responsibility of the church from heaven's vantage point. It was an odd picture, but I instantly understood the meaning. As I stood before the crowd, each one of them had a shovel. It was as if from heaven's viewpoint, there is a hole that needs to be unearthed through prayer and everyone has a shovel. Everyone is responsible.

What if the collective responsibility of us all is the equivalent of a hole that needs to be shoveled, but not a hole in the ground— a hole in the sky. Not a hole to get us to God, but a hole sufficient to release the experience of the kingdom of God from heaven to earth.

What if our prayers are the shovels? Who in the family has their back against the wall and their shovel at their feet, content to let everyone else do the digging? If this were an actual physical hole, we'd all look at inaction as unacceptable laziness. Once the sweat began to pop out on our foreheads, and our backs began to fatigue, we'd walk over and say, "In case you haven't noticed, the rest of us are digging. You have a shovel: Would you mind picking it up and doing your part?" This would be how the nice person would say it. Somebody a little saltier might add some colorful words and change the question into a command. Either way, you'd get the message. I'd like to fall somewhere in between and declare: "You are needed, and there is work to be done. Pick up your personal prayer movement like a shovel and begin!" God has given an invitation but also a mandate. Prayer stands before us as a profound opportunity, but make no mistake, it is also everyone's responsibility.

Most of us think of prayer in individual terms. Indeed, this book has been about learning to personally chase God. But the truth is, every personal relationship that we enjoy has a broader context, a bigger theater of life in which it plays out. In marriage we belong to families. In friendship we belong to any number of larger groups— schools, clubs, fraternities, sports teams. In citizenship we share the country of our origin. God has set a larger context for our relationship with him as well. In scripture we are called the Body of Christ. Though our prayer pursuits play out individually, we are members of a collective. We carry uniqueness and importance as an individual, but we also bear responsibility to the whole.

Think of it as a team— everybody has a role to play. When we all show up the team advances. Think of it as a farm family— everybody has the privilege of chores to complete before we are all free to move into recreation. As the Bride of Christ, there is a great recreation in our future— a great feast, an exclusive banquet. Who knows what is in store when God the Father unleashes his laughter and lavish gifts into a new heaven and a new earth? There are new names to be distributed and rewards to enjoy. But first, there is work to be done.

What keeps us stuck? What keeps our prayer shovel idle?

Consumer to Contender

Many are stuck in the posture of a consumer, content for the momentary high that comes from being around others who have been chasing God. This turns out to be an experience by way of run-off, crumbs from the table, prayer by hearsay rather than personal pursuit.

> "Consumer culture disciples us to change our external situation through purchasing to bring pleasure, meaning, and happiness to our inner world. Contending takes the opposite approach. Personal renewals begin in the hidden places, often driven by solitary prayer and self-examination, communion with God, fasting and the habits of secrecy, the uprooting of sinful patterns, and confessions."[39] (Reappearing Church, Mark Sayers)

It's time for the giant beliefs put forth in scripture and believed upon for centuries to come forth into our experience. Timeless truths must now become facts lived out. To see this our posture must shift from observing to engaging.

Let's embrace that this is not convenient. It is rearranging our life-processes to reach for something. It is the uncomfortable inward shift toward responsibility and reducing our options. It means that I stop blaming my lack of forward momentum on anything other than myself. It is the powerful shift away from multiple visions for my life, and the taking up of God's vision for my life, becoming the living interface where heaven meets earth.

It's time to grow wary of spiritual-sounding confessions that have no inconvenient action. Every shift in our schedule, every trade of some physical comfort for the pursuit of unseen things, every inch of surrender (our flesh beckoning for a stay of execution), every humble whisper of thanks must be rooted in real ticks of the clock, real movements of body and soul. Grand confessions in sacred moments lose their authenticity when not followed up by resolved habits.

The consumer to contender shift is the shift from amateur to professional, from a hobbyist to occupation, from fan to fanatic, from an idealist to a warrior. It is the shift from part-time to full-time, from sometimes to always. It is both confession and follow-through. Efforts will wobble and fall. But this is not three strikes, and you are out. This is dust off your failure and pray again.

Transformation makes inconvenient trades seem like a very small price to pay. Heaven begins to reshape earthly handicaps — I'm being re-made. It's here in the frontier of the heart that the deal is sealed. I have sought the Lord and found him. All the treasures of earth can now be sold I have found the One for whom I was made. Nothing else will do. My grip around the things of this world is loosening. A new DNA from heaven is slowly re-writing me. I can throw my lot in with the Apostle Paul who called himself, "A bondservant of Christ, doing the will of God from the heart." (Ephesians 6:6)

The presence of God is a team sport

I grew up watching my dad's teams play basketball. Year after year his teams were successful. The games were exciting, and winning is habit forming, but the work was done behind the scenes. Three-hour practices every day. The first forty-five minutes of drills were designed to build stamina and core skills. The simple fundamentals lead to wins.

But each player had to do their part. Everyone had to participate to learn their role and carry it faithfully. When a team comes together it's magical. Things previously impossible are now in reach. The presence of God and the Kingdom of Heaven at hand is a team sport — It is designed to exponentially thrive in community. But everybody must do his or her part. The presence of God was never meant to be carried alone. It has individual expressions and plenty of personal encounters, but all roads are designed to lead back to a community —a place where the presence of God can be experienced and discerned together.

Uzzah's death in 2 Samuel 6 proves that getting the community wrong is dangerous. We cannot afford the careless confusion about how God's presence is supposed to be carried. In this story we see King David excited about bringing the Ark of the Covenant back to Jerusalem. In his haste he borrows the strategy of the Philistines. He puts the Ark on a wooden cart pulled by oxen. When the oxen stumble, Uzzah reaches out to steady the ark. When he touches it, he dies on the spot. The burden and delight of God's presence is not meant to be carried by cart. God had already told them this in the Law. The weight of it cannot be pulled with any beast of burden.

But let's bring it closer to home. Neither can the presence of God be carried by church methodology, leadership initiatives, impressive facilities, the latest book, the newest song. All of these are important tools, but the presence of God can only be carried by people— people engaged in spiritual closeness with God. People who have bought into the inconvenient but rewarding cost of loving God. David should have avoided the "shortcut" of an ox cart. The prescription of God for carrying the Ark of the Covenant was two golden poles with four Levite priests (one at each corner, Exodus 25:13-14). In the ecosystem of God, the power of God's presence is most fully realized in community— a person at each corner. Each bearing the weight and responsibility of God with us.

When Everybody Prays

When everybody prays, God begins to move. That is the promise of scripture and the historical record of revival history. The scriptures thoroughly testify what happens when people authentically turn to God.

Renewal

Personal renewal is not the end goal, but it is a happy stop along the way. His plan to fill the earth begins with his intent to flood the individual. Revival awakening in the world is preceded by personal renewal in those who align themselves with the name of Jesus.

We see this play out in the apostle Peter's life. In the gospel of John, chapter 21, Peter is fresh off denying Jesus. He still seems a little lost. The disciples were in the days between Jesus with them and the Holy Spirit's arrival in Acts 2. In this twilight waiting, Peter goes back to fishing. All night with no success.

Frustrated and spent, Peter is analogous to how many of us feel in our lives. Nothing is working, we feel discouraged, and lacking a true north to set the course of our life. Jesus walks up to the shoreline. 100 yards away, Peter sees Jesus but doesn't recognize him. Pause at this point and consider that we are more like Peter than we admit. The Holy Spirit walks among the church unrecognized, our eyes unopened.

Jesus calls out:

"Cast your nets on the right side of the boat." A simple but inconvenient directive from Jesus to change course. To do life differently. Peter followed through and against all odds his nets filled with fish. Obedient action changes experience. We need our eyes opened to the presence of Jesus close at hand, but we cannot avoid his invitation to do things differently.

Though Peter was an expert fisherman, he listened to the invitation. The fish rushed into his net and his eyes opened. He recognized that it was Jesus. Again, pause at this point in the story and see it clearly. Peter was there to catch fish but when he recognized the presence of Jesus close by, every other design over his time shifted. Unwilling to wait for the boat to come to shore, he dove from the boat and swam to shore.

This is the attitude of renewal. I will not wait for the crowd to come with me. I will not delay one moment longer, I will leave behind all the conventions of protocol if I must, but I will get to Jesus. This resolve becomes the posture of all the ones who seek him in private until he is found. He who is the desire of every human heart must be treasured. It is the ones who have lost their civility, propriety, and left behind the safety of the boat who arrive first to the feet of Jesus. They arrive soaked, empty-handed, and with very little on. But they are profoundly ruined. Desperation has found its mark and everything else has been set to the side. The shortest distance to Jesus has been calculated and embraced. In a flash moment, the fixed value of the Matchless King has been brought nearby. The soul urgently whispers, "Not a moment to waste! Jump now!"

There is a giant caution here for all church leaders. Have you lost the value of the presence of the Matchless King? Have you hesitated, worried about appearances? Have you seen a direct route to where Jesus is standing but elected to take the strategically safe route to get to his feet? Have you let your desperation for his presence be restrained by your concern about what others would think? Have you felt the reflex to jump out of the boat but restrain yourself from the anxiety of whether others would follow you in such a radical swim? Afterall, doesn't it make more sense to stay in the boat and try to navigate everyone to shore in a civilized manner? Be very careful of your caution when it comes to God's presence.

Once Peter reached the shore, there in the presence of Jesus he was renewed. Little did he know that a revival changing the world would begin just a few weeks later. He had no idea that he would soon boldly stand right in the middle of it and declare the risen Jesus to all who would listen. Thousands would flow into the church community and give their lives to serve the King. Peter didn't know any of this. He only knew that Jesus in the room is the difference-maker. Whatever awkward displays of affection need to be made, it would all be worth it.

On this day, standing on the shore with Jesus, Peter was personally restored. I expect he remembered his swim toward Jesus for the rest of his life. In doing so perhaps he learned how to step into prayer with the same resolve— willing to push aside all comforts and conveniences for the incomparable treasure of the presence of God.

For every hungry soul who adopts the "I don't care what it costs me" zeal of Peter, personal renewal will come. And, like Peter, you don't know the details of what will happen next, but you can have the confidence that, like Peter, you will be powerfully standing in the purposes of God for your life. Bigger than you imagined, more costly than you anticipated, and his presence the guiding force over your life.

Revival Awakening

Revival is the same invasion of the kingdom of God as renewal, just on a different scale. In revival the life-giving presence of God begins to change churches, whole communities, entire regions and beyond. Renewal is an individual experience, but when revival erupts, history has shown that renewal becomes the common experience of the church and beyond (though there is nothing common about it). In fact, when it escapes the walls of the church and spills over into the region, country, or world, the name is upgraded to Awakening.

Prayer precedes. As the disciples gathered in Jerusalem in Acts 2, and every major revival awakening will attest, from a singular place of gathered prayer, a move of God goes viral and whole regions come under the holy influence of the presence of God.

None of us were around to hear Martin Luther's prayers, but we all live in the wake of them, for the Reformation changed the spiritual landscape of the planet forever.

None of us were present the day Jonathan Edwards preached **Sinners in the Hands of an Angry God** with people wailing in repentance before he could even finish. Neither did we get the privilege of seeing John Wesley ride into town, knowing that he'd cataloged hours of prayer on the back of his horse. None of us had the privilege of hearing the fiery preaching of George Whitfield. All these men of prayer were the sparks of the First Great Awakening (1730 – 1755). It swept through Great Britain and America like a fire.

Charles Finney was born the year after Wesley died and spanned one century to the next. He became the link not only from one century to the next, but also from the First Great Awakening to the Second. "When he opened his mouth, he was aiming a gun . . . in an age when there were no amplifiers or mass communications, he spearheaded a revival which literally altered the course of history."[40] It was the Second Great Awakening (1790 – 1840).

What does a Great Awakening look like? What will it look like when it comes again?

If we asked a room full of people, this question we'd likely get a wide variety of answers. Radical repentance, miracle healing, epidemic movements of communities returning to the Lord in salvation, demonic deliverance, inward wholeness, personal rescue, families restored, justice for the oppressed and cultural transformation: yes, to all the above. However, underneath all these things, there is the sustained experience of the presence of God. Beyond the narrow limits of a programmed service for Sunday morning church, the weight and significance of God descends upon a church, a city, a region, a nation, the world. Not just for a moment but continuing over a period of time.

The sustained experience of God's weighty presence marks revival. Whether it is a room or a region, when the glory of God settles, heavenly things begin to occur. The work of the Holy Spirit accelerates. Outcomes that normally would have taken years come to pass in moments. The culture of heaven settles into the atmosphere— the hardened sinner breaks, the profoundly sick healed, the tormented set free, the broken made whole, the depressed filled with joy unspeakable. Do not imagine that this is an orderly event or business as usual. No, the whole point is that it is NOT business as usual. God is dwelling and we are attending to his presence. How could anything remain normal?

Two weeks ago, I met three other friends at 4:30 am and made a trip to Asbury University in Kentucky. There is an outpouring of God's Spirit happening there and spreading to other college campuses as I'm sitting here writing. I didn't know what to expect. There would be crowds from all over the country, for in our technological age word spreads fast, and people are hungry for God. Me too. Cautiously expectant. Unwilling to sit on the sidelines of whatever God was up to— I went.

We arrived six hours later and what I experienced was not normal. We got there forty-five minutes before the doors were supposed to open and there was already a line 150 yards long standing in cold rain. After five minutes of standing in line, my heart began to squeeze, and I felt tears trying to burn out of my eyes. Though my outside skin was getting colder, my heart was warming up. I wasn't even close to the front door of the 100-year-old Hughes Auditorium, but I could sense that this was holy ground.

I don't know about you, but I cry at graduations, weddings, the opening of the World Series —wherever humanity gathers to honor someone or something they love. This was like that feeling but more. People from all over the country gathering just to honor God and give him the worship due his name. My heart grew a couple of sizes at the sight of this, and we hadn't even sung the first song.

We got inside and sat in the row that would be our home for the next eight hours. Lo-fi worship from students began to humbly stream from the stage. Once the building was full, a spokesperson took the stage. What he said perfectly captured the essence of my whole experience at Asbury: **"If you are looking for a show there is not one, only space to abide."** Then he added, **"It's just the ordinary, holy love of God."**

Truly there was nothing to see. But plenty to experience, for it seemed to me that the presence of God rested upon the crowd. Tender, powerful waves of the Holy Spirit washing across the room. Undeniable.

Even still, I began to have leadership thoughts. An unwelcome interruption. "Where is this going?" "What are we building here?" Then the voice of the Spirit shushed me with the simple answer— "The love of God is an end in itself. It is the perfect destination of the human soul." Nothing else needs to be done.

I settled in and enjoyed Jesus for eight beautiful hours— again, not normal.

Scripture and revival-awakening history conspire against our weak notions of normalcy. In scripture we see the atmosphere around God's throne, and it is everything that normal is not. We do best if we exit the religious evaluation lounge and let our hearts burn with desire for God. When we draw boundaries around what God can and cannot do, we do not shrink him, we shrink the possibilities of his work among us. The importance here is that revival awakenings have historically brought about spiritual manifestations that are unusual. Usually troubling to the doubly religious. We should resist being close-minded and prepare to be resolutely unoffendable.

Some may object, "Aren't you worried about false manifestations through human emotion?" No. Human error, fleshly indulgence, and even demonic mischief is certain. Jesus warned us that the wheat and the tare would grow side by side in the church. Revival will not change that fact. But neither does the prescription of Jesus change. "Let both of them grow together until harvest." (Matthew 13:30, NIV)

The Knowledge of the Glory of the Lord

When scripture refers to "the knowledge of the glory of the Lord," it is knowledge that is bigger than the exchange of information. It is knowledge that is gained through experience. We may know many things about God, but it is a different day when those things become personal experience. Like the president of Asbury College said of the revival that broke out on their campus back in 1970:

"Things that were simply tradition became reality. Things that were human vocabulary became human experience; things that had been transmitted head-to-head now became living reality."[41]

Most of our objections to spiritual things that we don't understand are rooted in pride and control. Pride never releases the full potential of any relationship. Humility makes room for things previously unknown. We must steer ourselves toward the humble admission that our "head knowledge" about God is limited and that our experiential knowledge is equally valuable. In relationships, knowledge born in experience is superior to mere knowledge.

I knew many things that were supposed to be true about my wife before I married her – things her friends said, comments her mother made, etc. Then I married her. Now I can confirm and deny many things, but it is not hearsay, it is personal experience. As it turns out, this is exactly the kind of knowledge that God invites us into. This kind of knowledge is never complete. I've been married for 36 years and while I know my wife better than anyone else, I could never claim that I've got her figured out. How much truer is this with God?

God will fill the earth with the glory of the knowledge of himself, but not so that we can claim we've finally figured him out. No, but rather, that we would fall deeper into the mystery of his person. Further fascination with each new layer.

"For the earth will be filled with the knowledge of the glory of the Lord as the waters cover the sea" (Habakkuk 2:14)

The Prepared Church

It can be argued that God sovereignly releases revival awakenings over geographic regions in his own timing and at his sovereign discretion. Whether this is true or not doesn't change how the local church should be chasing. If you are wondering when God would be willing to release a powerful move of his Spirit, stop looking at the calendar and start looking at your wristwatch. Why not build the culture and experience of the church around the ripe belief that God is ready to move now. Our lamps filled with oil and our eyes watchful and ready.

Devoted to His Presence

One Sunday night many years ago, I was sitting through another church service listening to the pastor make his way through his sermon. All of sudden, right in the middle of his teaching, he paused. He looked out over the congregation and said, "God's here."

I was young. In my 20's, I think. But I knew enough about the presence of God that I paused to notice. He was right. There was a weighty presence moving into the room. The pastor closed his notes and said, "When God enters the room, we yield the room to him." His sermon was abandoned, and the room became an active theater of the Holy Spirit's ministry. Full of mystery, beauty, and power. I was marked by the experience.

I'm not suggesting that every gathering of the church has to have holy interruptions, but shouldn't the presence of God be the sustained experience of the church? This may seem misguided to some. Perhaps too subjective to be a standard to reckon upon. However, as I have testified repeatedly, the presence of God marks every atmosphere where the Holy Spirit is invited to walk. And the church that is willing to prioritize God's presence above every other agenda can have this atmosphere continually. It's very hard to do given all the other competing agendas of church growth, discipleship, and leadership expansion. We may have our eye on opening the next campus while an attentiveness to God's presence dulls and leaks away through the back door. This is not a problem to solve but a tension to wholeheartedly manage. Growth is good, building disciples is a must, leadership is required to get things done, the next campus is a worthwhile goal. However, the church which guards the emphasis of God's presence is positioned to be empowered for all of these pursuits.

I must remember the lessons of Martha and Mary. Martha, busy and distracted, trying to get things accomplished. Mary devoted and attentive to the presence of Jesus in the room. In this tension Jesus casts the deciding vote, "Martha, Martha, you are anxious and troubled about many things, but one thing is necessary. Mary has chosen the good portion, which will not be taken away from her." (Luke 10:41, 42, ESV) Jesus didn't say that Martha and all her agendas should be put away. He simply pointed out that nothing is more important than his presence in the room.

I can also use the Mary— Martha tension as an excuse to not get anything done. Not growing, lax in my attention to detail, using my pursuit of God's presence as a rational to not move forward. In essence, this posture banishes Martha in an effort to preserve the devotion of Mary. This is not the answer either.

It is not an "either—or" problem, it is a "both—and" tension. The practical excellence of Martha must be maintained, but we always give first devotion to the risen Savior alive in the room. We will never sustain this guarding of God's presence until we wholeheartedly embrace an emphasis upon it.

"In most Christian churches the Spirit is quite entirely overlooked. Whether He is present or absent makes no real difference to anyone . . . Our neglect of the doctrine of the blessed Third Person has had and is having serious consequences. For doctrine is dynamite. It must have emphasis sufficiently sharp to detonate it before its power is released. The doctrine of the Spirit is buried dynamite. Its power awaits discovery and use by the Church . . . The Holy Spirit cares not at all whether we write Him into our creeds . . . He awaits our emphasis."[42]

The church who invites sustained renewal and revival must cede every other emphasis as secondary to the presence of God before the church.

A Church Rooted in Prayer

Church culture doesn't just happen. It is formed from the things you repeatedly say and do. It takes shape around where you spend your money and time— constructed from the values that your team carries in the center of its heart. Built one brick at a time from a clear and intended target. One thing is for certain, prayer will never take a central place in the culture of your church without constant vigilance.

Just like the personal prayer habits that you may put in place, churches can similarly make plans. Prayer and worship nights, seven days of morning or evening prayer. At our church, we even did 150 days of praying from the Psalms. We used online technology to pray from a Psalm every day until we prayed through the whole book. There is no magic in the initiative that you choose; it just matters that you demonstrate the value that you declare with real action.

Church leaders can set these initiatives in place as they map out their calendar year. However, if you add no new processes or events to your calendar, you can still migrate everything you are already doing into an ethos of God's presence by prayer. I said earlier that the secret to prayer is that prayer is not about prayer, it is about connecting to God's presence. Similarly, the secret to the culture of a church is not only about the events that are on the calendar, but also about the kingdom reflexes that are being cultivated in the heart of the church. Kingdom reflexes are biases that reflect how the church responds in an ongoing manner, regardless of what events are on the calendar.

A Reflex towards Gathered Prayer

There is exponential potential in gathered prayer that will never be available in private prayer. Don't get it twisted. There are things that only happen in private prayer. But churches that are powerfully rooted in prayer are churches who uncompromisingly guard the commitment of gathered prayer. It may be inside of the services that you already have, but the pause and prominence of God's place in the room must get authentic focus. Simply put, God does things in rooms full of people in pursuit of him that will not happen anywhere else.

A Reflex towards Inconvenience and Cost

Our natural instincts are to avoid inconvenience and costly investments of time. Churches who have a commitment to gathered prayer embrace a reflex toward the reality of inconvenience. In other words, the church rooted in prayer gives up the foolish notion that the gathered prayer will ever be shoe-horned into a convenient place in the schedule, or inside the perfectly balanced program nestled in planning center.

Churches need to flip their perspective and embrace the costly inconvenience. The church which can learn to embrace inconvenient cost as an advantage is a powerful church. It's like the disciples who were beaten for the testimony of Jesus and then went their way rejoicing that they'd been counted worthy to suffer for his name. (Acts 5:41)

In the early days of my time at 12Stone Church, I worked a full-time job in sales and only part-time at the church. I worked all day on Saturday in sales, came home and ate dinner, helped put three young kids to bed and then went to 9:15pm prayer at the church. In the early days of this commitment, I found great resistance in my heart every Saturday night. I was tired and I faced a full day ahead on Sunday. But I would nevertheless go in the conviction that it was important.

What I learned pretty quickly was how powerfully God responds to love expressed in an inconvenient manner. I walked into prayer almost with a chip on my shoulder. But as soon as I walked into the building, it was like he was waiting for me. He changed everything. One moment I felt like I was going to pray out of obligation. Then in almost a blink of an eye, my gratitude and affection towards God began to flow. Saturday prayer became the indispensable piece of my week that prepared my heart for Sunday church.

In the due course of time, I learned that inconvenience, when embraced, became an ally. The church that wants to stay rooted in prayer will have to grow a reflex towards costly inconvenience.

A Reflex towards Hands On Prayer
A powerful shift happened in our church when we began to make room to pray for people one-on-one. The intent is to lead them into an encounter with the presence of God for he always seems ready to meet those who humbly come and ask for help.

This kind of praying seems to easily get lost in the shadow of other priorities. But the more emphasis the church puts upon it, the greater the results. It requires people who will submit to training to become effective in leading people into encounters with God. It also requires enough time so that you can pray with people at the speed of love. Listening to them. Discerning how best to pray.

A Reflex towards the Present Tense
When I stepped into the role of leading the prayer movement, I decided to meet with the top leaders on our staff. They were quick meetings where I simply asked them to examine their own practice and conviction of prayer. Each one was super gracious and completely on board. The last of these meetings was with Dan Reiland who was serving as our Executive Pastor. Dan is super sharp and as our meeting was finishing up, he asked me a question that I wasn't prepared to answer. He said, "Chris, this all sounds great and I'm completely on board and supportive. But can you give me one practical example of something I can do that is different from what I'm already doing?"

On the inside, I froze. I was merely lobbying for his general support. I hadn't prepared specific examples. But even as I felt like I was freezing on the inside, I heard myself say on the outside, "Yes! I think it would be helpful if we all began to pay attention to the tense in which we are praying. We are too much in the habit of praying for things that we want to see happen in the future. Nothing wrong with that, but I believe we'd see a powerful shift in perspective if we'd begin to address God in the present tense." He smiled and said, "Wow! Thank you, that was helpful."

The truth is it felt like the Holy Spirit totally bailed me out. I felt like I was hearing that thought for the first time too. But it has become an important leadership reflex for me. One of God's primary attributes is that he is always present tense. Like I said earlier, "my favorite moment is now." The church powerfully rooted in prayer is the church who is constantly looking for God in the present moment.

A Reflex towards Unplanned Interruptions
In September of 2019, my pastor got a leading from the Holy Spirit to invite anyone who wanted prayer to come back to the church on Sunday night at 6pm. His commitment was that however many people showed up he would personally pray with everyone.

He made the offer and then asked me to join him. We didn't know whether it would be five or five hundred, we just knew that we were going to take our time and pray over each one like they were the only one.

That's exactly what we did. We prayed for people from 6pm till 4:15am the following morning. Wow! What a night that was.

Who would stick around for two hours to receive prayer, much less ten hours? The answer is– people immersed in God's presence. The atmosphere that night was so rich with an awareness of God's presence that everyone could sense it. There were at least 275 people in the room, everyone stayed reverent and prayerful the whole night.

God met people in prayer. Powerful encounters with God took place. I felt so privileged to be there. By the time 4am arrived, my back and feet were wrecked, but I didn't care. The air in that room felt like it was piped in straight from heaven. In the presence of God, all the normal rules change.

The point?

Part of what it means to be rooted in prayer is that you are interruptible. God has your permission to interfere with your plans, and to initiate his own. Most of us agree with this idea in concept, but fewer of us are ready for a real-life interruption.

Let's begin to wrap up our journey together by coming back to the place where all prayer begins. A personal decision to say yes to a relationship with God.

Where are You?

The first and shortest question in the scriptures is the word "ay"? It appears three chapters into Genesis. It is the question God posed to

Adam and Eve, "Where are you?" God is not trying to geo-locate Adam and Eve. He wouldn't be God if he didn't actually know where they were. The question is an invitation to come out from hiding and know God. That first and shortest question still hovers over my life today. As I chase God in prayer, I am setting in motion my response to his appeal. Every expression of honest prayer is me coming out of hiding. It is me saying "Yes! Here I am!"

Building a life rooted in prayer is how I aim my heart upon the outcome that God's presence will prevail and fill the earth. The fast train of time that will end with Jesus's reign on earth begins with Jesus's reign over me— personally, privately and through prayer.

Until this glorious outcome is achieved, may I be found faithful. Fortifying my heart day upon day, one relational brick laid upon the next, yielding layers of transformation and years of personal experience. But all along, Jesus is becoming the treasure of my life.

As we pack up our short journey together, let's boil it down to something so relationally simple that none of us could miss the point: **When God is chased, he gets caught.**

The day for radical seeking of God is now.

Invocation

Next Step:
Join Jesus and take up your place in his world-wide movement.

Scripture:
Therefore, since we are surrounded by such a great cloud of witnesses, let us throw off everything that hinders and the sin that so easily entangles. And let us run with perseverance the race marked out for us. (Hebrews 12:1, NIV)

Quote:
A faith-filled person is always the last one standing in the ring and the first one kneeling in obscurity. (Kris Vallaton)

Our primary call is not ministry— it's intimacy. We don't pray before we work, prayer is the work, then God works. — **Pastor Vance Pittman, Hope Church, Las Vegas**

Prayer:
Father, I long to see the day of your glory. May the walls of my chest become the keeper of a sacred conversation— a dual dialogue bent toward the renewal of all things. May the chambers of my soul be filled with the whispers of your Spirit. May my spirit rise to shout in return!

Draw your church to yourself and set within her a flame of fire that no flood could extinguish.

1. A metaphor I first heard from Pastor Kevin Myers (12Stone Church) in 2006.

2. Coach Jim Morgan: 13 years East Bend HS, 17 years East Surry HS-- 606 Wins / 313 Losses

3. John Wesley, The Journal of John Wesley (Lexington, KY, 2012), 57.

4. Charles G. Finney, Memoirs of Rev. Charles G. Finney (New York: A.S. Barnes & Company, 1896) 20-21

5. Al Szymanski (Director). (2019). Garth: The Road I'm On. [Documentary]. Endeavor Production Documentary

6. Tomorrow, Track 5, Charles Strouse and Martin Chamin, Annie: The Broadway Musical 30th Anniversary Cast Recording, 2008.

7. C.S. Lewis Institute, America's Great Revivals, (Minneapolis, Minnesota: Bethany House Publishers, 2004)

8. A.W. Tozer, The Divine Conquest, (First Living Books edition, 1995) 9.

9. Charles Spurgeon, Morning by Morning, (Grand Rapids, Michigan, 2008)

10. Pastor Kevin Myers, 12Stone Church, Men's prayer gathering, 2016

11. C.S. Lewis, The Lion, the Witch and the Wardrobe, (New York Macmillan 1950) 41-42

12. My paraphrase of what Jesus said in Mat. 6: 1-5

13. Again, my paraphrase of Luke 19:13-14

14. C.S. Lewis, The Chronicles of Narnia: The Silver Chair (HarperCollins e-books) 18-21

15. A.W. Tozer, The Pursuit of God, (Christian Publications Inc. 1993, P. 8)

16. Gary Waksman (Director). (210). Four Days in October, (30 for 30 documentary), ESPN

17. A.W. Tozer, The Divine Conquest, (First Living Books edition, 1995) 7.

18. Pastor Kevin Myers, June 2019, 12Stone Church, Sermon Prayer Unscripted

19. John Milton, Paradise Lost, (Entreacacias, SL, 2020) Book IV, Line 73

20. John 4: 10-15, paraphrase of the conversation of Jesus with the women at the well based on the NIV

21. Mark Twain, The Adventures of Huckleberry Finn, (WaldenBooks, 1983) 144

22. A.W. Tozer, The Pursuit of God, (Christian Publications Inc. 1993) 69

23. A.W. Tozer, The Divine Conquest, (First Living Books edition, 1995) 8.

24. Mark Sayers, Reappearing Church, 2019 (Moody Publishers, 2019) 9

25. The A.W. Tozer, The Pursuit of God, (Christian Publications Inc. 1993) 13

26. Pastor Jon Tyson, Church of the City, New York, sermon "Crying Out: That you may Pray" 2020.

27. A.W. Tozer, How to be Filled with the Holy Spirit, (Christian Publications 2001) 35

28. A.J. Gordon, The Twofold Life, (Copyright: Boston, Howard Gannet) 10-12

29. Exodus 13:21 Just after the crossing of the Red Sea

30. V. Raymond Edman, They Found the Secret, (1960, 1984 by Zondervan) 72-73

31. Raymond Edman, They Found the Secret, (1960, 1984 by Zondervan) 76

32. "Prayer Unscripted" Sermon, 12Stone Church, 2019

33. Bill Johnson, Dreaming with God, (Destiny Image Publishers, Inc.) 23

34. Eugene Kim (2014) businessinsider.com, article: The 14 fastest unicorns to reach 1 billion. [online] Available: https://www.businessinsider.com/fastest-startups-to-1-billion-valuation-2015-8

35. Olivia Harrison (2011) Wisdom [online] Available: https://www.youtube.com/watch?v=F6X9EyQdbf0

36. John Milton, Paradise Lost, (Entreacacias, SL, 2020) Book IV

37. 41. Henry Alford, The works of John Donne (London: John W. Parker, West Strand. 1839) Vol. 2

38. Pete Greig, Dirty Glory, (Tyndale House Publishers, Inc. 2016)

39. Mark Sayers, Reappearing Church, (Moody Publishers, 2019) 141

40. Winkie Pratney, Revival, (Whitaker House)116

41. Dr. Dennis Kinlaw, (1970) A Revival Account: Asbury 1970 [online] Available: https://www.youtube.com/watch?v=7qOqitIKUNs&t=1201s

42. A.W. Tozer, God's Pursuit of Man, (Pennsylvania, Second Wing Spread Publishers Edition, 2007) 61

About the Author

Chris has almost forty years of local church ministry experience. Most of those years as a worship pastor where he built teams, coached them and weekly led the church into God's presence. The last six years the emphasis has shifted to presence-centered leadership and prayer-based approaches to growing churches and building disciples — there is nothing more important or powerful than how a church engages the presence of God.

He lives on a small farm in North Georgia with his wife, Mary Anne. There he chases grand kids, chickens, and loves to garden – building disciples and helping churches grow one conversation at a time.

chrismorgan.co
cmo@12stone.com
coachcmo268@gmail.com

Made in the USA
Columbia, SC
22 July 2023